The Echoing Wood of Theodore Roethke

PRINCETON ESSAYS IN LITERATURE

For a listing of all titles, see page 175.

The Echoing Wood of
Theodore Roethke

"I hear my echo in the echoing wood."
—ROETHKE

Jenijoy La Belle

Princeton University Press
Princeton, New Jersey

Published by Princeton University Press, Princeton, New Jersey
In the United Kingdom: Princeton University Press, Guildford, Surrey

Library of Congress Cataloging in Publication Data will be found on the last printed page of this book

Publication of this book has been aided by The Andrew W. Mellon Foundation

This book has been composed in Linotype Janson

Printed in the United States of America by Princeton University Press, Princeton, New Jersey

For

my Mother and Father

"for love, for Love's sake"

Acknowledgments

"We never enter Alone."
ROETHKE

In preparing this book I have gained much from previous studies of Roethke's poetry, particularly Karl Malkoff's *Theodore Roethke: An Introduction to the Poetry* (1966) and Richard A. Blessing's *Theodore Roethke's Dynamic Vision* (1974). Beatrice Roethke Lushington and the staff of the Roethke Collection, University of Washington, Seattle, have been most helpful in making available to me manuscript materials and books from Roethke's library. I am deeply indebted to a number of friends who have read my manuscript and offered encouragement and numerous improvements. I wish especially to thank Richard A. Blessing, Robert N. Essick, and Roy Harvey Pearce. The initial inspiration for this study came from my classes with Roethke at the University of Washington (1962-1963), and the continuing research was guided by Professor Pearce.

Many of the ideas in this book first appeared in my doctoral thesis "Theodore Roethke and Tradition: 'The Pure Serene of Memory in One Man,'" 1969, which has been available through University Microfilms Inc. Some of these ideas, particularly those on traditional allusions in Roethke's poetry, also appeared in my article of the same name in *Northwest Review*. Rosemary Sullivan, in her book, *The Garden Master: Style and Identity in the Poetry of Theodore Roethke* (University of Washington Press, 1975), has made good use of these materials in a work dealing mainly with Roethke's evolution as a poet. Since this book appears considerably after Professor Sullivan's, I want to insure that there should be no misunderstandings as to the genesis of various passages from my original thesis that are preserved here.

I am grateful to Beatrice Roethke Lushington and the University of Washington Library Manuscripts Collection for permission to quote thirteen lines from the notebooks of Theodore Roethke; to the University of Washington Press for permission to quote from *On the Poet and His Craft: Selected Prose of Theodore Roethke* (copyright © 1965 by Beatrice Roethke as administratrix of the estate of Theodore Roethke), and from *Selected Letters of Theodore Roethke* (copyright © 1968 by Beatrice Roethke as administratrix of the estate of Theodore Roethke), both edited by Ralph J. Mills, Jr.; to Doubleday and Company, Inc. for permission to quote "Death Piece," "No Bird," copyright 1934 by Theodore Roethke, "Feud," copyright 1935 by Theodore Roethke, "Long Live The Weeds," copyright 1936 by Theodore Roethke, "Interlude," "The Adamant," copyright 1938 by Theodore Roethke, "On The Road To Woodlawn," "Mid-Country Blow," "Open House," "The Premonition," copyright 1941 by Theodore Roethke, "The Minimal," copyright 1942 by Theodore Roethke, "Dolor," copyright 1943 Modern Poetry Association, Inc., "Night Crow," copyright 1944 Saturday Review Association, Inc., "Carnations," "Child On Top Of A Greenhouse," "Moss-Gathering," "Weed Puller," copyright 1946 Editorial Publications, Inc., "Old Florist," 1946 Harper & Brothers, "The Flight," "The Long Alley," "The Lost Son," "The Shape Of The Fire," copyright 1947 by Theodore Roethke, "Cuttings (later)," copyright 1948 by Theodore Roethke, "Unfold! Unfold!," copyright 1949 by Theodore Roethke, "Where Knock Is Open Wide," "I Cry, Love! Love!," copyright 1950 by Theodore Roethke, "Bring The Day!," "O Lull Me, Lull Me," "Sensibility! O La!," copyright 1951 by Theodore Roethke, "O, Thou Opening, O," copyright 1952 by Theodore Roethke, "The Dance," copyright 1952 The Atlantic Monthly Company, "The Vigil," "The Wraith," copyright by Theodore Roethke, "I Knew A Woman," copyright © 1954 by Theodore Roethke, "The Dream," "First Meditation," copyright © 1955 by Theodore Roethke, "Slug," copyright © 1955 by New Republic Inc., "I'm Here," copyright © 1956 by Theodore Roethke, "I Waited," copyright © 1956 Kenyon College, "What Can I Tell My Bones?," copyright © 1957 by Theodore Roethke, "Fourth Meditation," "Pure Fury," "The Swan," copyright © 1958 by Theodore Roethke, "Her Becoming," copyright © 1958 Botteghe Oscure, "In Evening Air," "Meditation At Oyster River," copyright © 1960 by Beatrice Roethke, Administratrix of the Estate of Theodore Roethke, "The Lizard," "Otto," copyright © 1961 by Beatrice Roethke, Administratrix of the Estate of Theodore Roethke, "The Far Field," "The Longing," "Once More, The Round," copyright © 1962 by Beatrice Roethke, Administratrix of the Estate of Theodore Roethke, "The Abyss," "The Meadow Mouse," "The Pike," "The Right Thing," copyright © 1963 by Beatrice Roethke, Administratrix of the Estate of Theodore Roethke, "Heard In A Violent Ward," copyright © 1964 by Beatrice Roethke, Administratrix of the Estate of Theodore Roethke, all from *The Collected Poems of Theodore Roethke*. Reprinted by special arrangement with Doubleday and Company, Inc.; to City Lights Books to quote three lines from *Howl and Other Poems* by Allen Ginsberg (copyright © 1956, 1959 by Allen Ginsberg); to Viking Press for permission to quote from *The Complete Poems of D. H. Lawrence*, edited by Vivian de Sola Pinto and Warren Roberts (copyright © 1964, 1971 by Angelo Ravagli and C. M. Weekley, Executors of the Estate of Frieda Lawrence Ravagli) and from *The Rainbow* by D. H. Lawrence (copyright 1943 by Frieda Lawrence); to New York University Press for permission to quote from Walt Whitman, *Leaves of Grass: Comprehensive Reader's Edition*, edited by Harold Blodgett and Scully Bradley (copyright © 1965 by New York University); to Little, Brown and Company to quote seven lines from *The Complete Poems of Emily Dickinson*, edited by Thomas H. Johnson (copyright 1929 by Martha Dickinson

Bianchi, copyright © 1957 by Mary L. Hampson); to Harvard University Press and the Trustees of Amherst College to quote from *The Poems of Emily Dickinson*, edited by Thomas H. Johnson, Cambridge, Massachusetts, the Belknap Press of Harvard University Press (copyright © 1951, 1955 by the President and Fellows of Harvard College); to Harcourt Brace Jovanovich for permission to quote from T. S. Eliot, *Collected Poems 1909-1962* (copyright © 1934, 1936 by Harcourt, Brace & World, Inc.); to Macmillan Company for permission to quote from *The Collected Poems of William Butler Yeats* (copyright © 1933 by Macmillan Publishing Co., Inc., renewed 1961 by Bertha Georgie Yeats).

I wish to thank the following journals for permission to reprint material appearing in my articles listed with each journal. *Northwest Review*, "Theodore Roethke and Tradition: 'The Pure Serene of Memory in One Man' " (Summer 1971); *The Explicator*, "Roethke's I Knew A Woman" (October 1973); *Ball State University Forum*, "Martyr to a Motion Not His Own: Theodore Roethke's Love Poems" (Spring 1975); *Concerning Poetry*, "Theodore Roethke's Dancing Masters in 'Four for Sir John Davies' " (Fall 1975); *Modern Language Quarterly*, "Theodore Roethke's 'Lost Son': From Archetypes to Literary History" (Spring 1976); *Blake Studies*, "William Blake, Theodore Roethke, and Mother Goose: The Unholy Trinity" (Summer 1976).

J.L.B.

Contents

	Acknowledgments	vii
	Introduction	3
I	Conscious Imitation	7
II	Sympathetic Imitation	24
III	A Widening Sensibility	51
IV	Archetypes of Tradition	84
V	A Motion Not His Own	104
VI	Meditations	126
VII	A Storm of Correspondences	141
	Afterword	165
	Index	169

The Echoing Wood of Theodore Roethke

Introduction

"Our tendency [is] to insist, when we praise a poet, upon those aspects of his work in which he least resembles anyone else. . . . We dwell with satisfaction upon the poet's difference from his predecessors . . . whereas if we approach a poet without this prejudice we shall often find that not only the best, but the most individual parts of his work may be those in which the dead poets, his ancestors, assert their immortality most vigorously."[1]

Ever since the publication of these words of T. S. Eliot in his "Tradition and the Individual Talent" (1919), critics have taken an increasing interest in the relationship between modern poetry and the works of the past toward which it reaches for sustenance. Eliot's own statements have themselves become part of a tradition, insisting that poetry cannot be written *in vacuo*. Yet the modern situation—so the argument goes—allows the poet no body of generally accepted meanings or purposeful rhetoric that he can use in full confidence of being understood. The poet must therefore discover and in a sense determine that tradition to which he can refer himself and his reader in order to provide the sense of community that is a necessary condition for poetry. This study considers the ways one such poet, Theodore Roethke, defined and created in his poetry that cultural tradition in which he felt himself to be living and writing. Further, my concern will be with the ways in which an understanding of Roethke's explicit and implicit creation of a tradition for himself is essential for the proper interpretation of his work.

Stephen Spender, in his essay "The Objective Ego," writes that "The poems most uniquely Roethke are those in *The*

[1] T. S. Eliot, *Selected Essays* (New York: Harcourt, Brace & World, 1960), pp. 3-4.

Lost Son and Other Poems and *Praise to the End!* In these the originality is very 'far gone,' so much so that, a little further, and the reader would lose contact with the poet. It is difficult to think of poems which derive more completely from the fusion of the poet's isolated sensibility with a very solitary experience, going back to his childhood in the greenhouses. . . ."[2] A close reading of the poems in the two collections cited by Spender reveals, however, that Roethke's sensibility is not "isolated," but is continually referring the reader to a heritage of poetry that at once defines the cultural ambience in which the work must be understood and aids the poet in moving beyond "solitary experience" to the creation of transpersonal experience. In "The Lost Son," for example, Roethke writes

> Where do the roots go? . . .
> Ask the mole, he knows.

The poet in fact is referring us back to another poem, Blake's *Book of Thel*, as an unmistakable guidepost for our reading of his poem. Indeed, every title in Part 1 of *Praise to the End!* is a direct quotation from one of those poets who helped to shape this sequence. One's understanding of this collection, as well as of many of Roethke's other poems, is radically changed once the specific elements of Roethke's tradition from which the poems spring are revealed. Thus a knowledge of sources is not just a historical footnote to our reading of Roethke's poetry, but an integral part of our total experience of his work.

I have tried in what follows to consider why Roethke saw himself to be writing in the tradition of certain poems and poets, how he established his own cultural tradition, and what effect this tradition had upon his achievement as a poet. I have attempted to avoid defining tradition as simply a collection of vague, generalized influences and styles. I have

[2] Stephen Spender, "The Objective Ego," *Theodore Roethke: Essays on the Poetry*, ed. Arnold Stein (Seattle: University of Washington Press, 1965), p. 8.

kept in mind Roethke's warning in his essay "How to Write Like Somebody Else," which begins, "A good deal of nonsense has been written about 'influence' in modern poetry."[3] Thus I have tried to avoid those abstract critical commonplaces ("Eliotesque," "Audenesque," "classical") which verge on the nonsensical when not supported by clear and specific evidence—hard, particular data—for their relevance to particular poems. The method of this study, I like to think, grows out of Roethke's own approach to poetry. In the classroom he rarely talked about historical trends and aesthetic principles; rather, he constantly pointed out to his students good lines as models for their efforts as poets. We see this approach coming to bear again and again in his own poetry. Placing Roethke's poems in a tradition rather than simply exclaiming over their novelty fulfills an important critical function: as T. S. Eliot writes in his introduction to *The Sacred Wood*, "it is part of the business of the critic to preserve tradition—where a good tradition exists."[4] Just as Eliot is one of the best guides for the critic of Roethke's sense of tradition, he was also his mentor in the development of that tradition. Although Roethke's shrewd comments on Eliot's techniques as a poet are often negative, Eliot's authoritative dicta on a poet's use of the past are a hovering presence throughout Roethke's career.

Some critics of Roethke's poetry have offered general discussions and evaluations without a close consideration of the kinds of poetry he specifically—in his titles—tells us he is writing ("Prayer," "Elegy," "Plaint," "Once More, the Round," *Meditations of an Old Woman*, and *Sequence, Sometimes Metaphysical*), and others neglect to consider the sources of those of Roethke's titles which direct us to the full context in which his poems should be read. The roots of

[3] *On the Poet and His Craft: Selected Prose of Theodore Roethke*, ed. Ralph J. Mills, Jr. (Seattle: University of Washington Press, 1965), p. 61.

[4] T. S. Eliot, *The Sacred Wood: Essays on Poetry and Criticism* (London: Barnes & Noble, 1920), p. xv.

Roethke's poetry are not to be found only in the soil of his father's greenhouses and gardens in Michigan, where he passed his childhood. Roethke's roses come from far more "floral establishments" than those of his father: there are also Dante, Yeats, and Eliot. Likewise, the soil to which he transplants these flowers comes as much from Blake's "Vales of Har" as from the Saginaw Valley. Just as a knowledge about a poet's life may give us a fuller context for the understanding of his work, so too a knowledge of sources can be helpful—and indeed with Roethke is essential—to understand both what he wrote and how he wrote it. Further, the changes in Roethke's response to his literary past are at the heart of his changing methods and interests. The growth of this poet's mind as he moves from his early lyrics to his final sequences is concomitant with his evolving relationship with his tradition, from his rage against the past to "the pure serene of memory." Indeed this phrase from "The Far Field" demonstrates Roethke's reliance on tradition—echoing, as it does, both Gray and Keats.[5]

Even the sympathetic reader may feel at times burdened by the number of specific comparisons upon which this study depends. But, as Blake warns us, we must attend to minute particulars in order to avoid the pitfall of abstraction. Even though a few of the sources proposed here are tentative, I hope that the accumulated weight of evidence will satisfactorily counter objections to this approach at the level of principle. Or, if there are disagreements with some of my readings of Roethke's poems based on a knowledge of the tradition, this study still gives the basic evidence upon which different interpretations may be founded. Yet a cataloguing of sources is hardly the *raison d'être* of this book; rather, it is the means to a greater end—not only interpretations of the poems themselves but a portrait of Roethke's mind engaged with the past to create in the present.

[5] See Gray's "Full many a gem of purest ray serene" in his "Elegy Written in a Country Churchyard" and Keats's "Yet did I never breathe its pure serene" in "On First Looking into Chapman's Homer."

I

Conscious Imitation

"In any quest for identity today—or any day," wrote Roethke, "we run up inevitably against this problem: What to do with our ancestors? I mean it as an ambiguity: both the literal or blood, and the spiritual ancestors. Both, as we know, can overwhelm us. The devouring mother, the furious papa. And if we're trying to write, the Supreme Masters."[1] This "problem" as defined by Roethke in 1963, the last year of his life, was exactly the one with which he was struggling thirty years earlier while writing the poems for his first volume, *Open House* (1941). He was desperately "trying to write," but he was frightened and awed by the presence of the great poets of the past:

> Corruption reaps the young; you dread
> The menace of ancestral eyes; . . .
>
> ("Feud," CP 4)[2]

He figured the relationship between modern poets and past poets as an "ancient feud," and felt that he would not be able to create poetry until he had somehow vanquished his literary forefathers: "The spirit starves/Until the dead have been subdued." He had yet to learn how to transform past poets from enemies into allies.

Another of his earliest poems, "Sale," also involves what one inherits from the past. In both "Feud" and "Sale"

[1] "On 'Identity,'" *On the Poet and His Craft*, p. 23.

[2] *The Collected Poems of Theodore Roethke* (New York: Doubleday, 1966), p. 4. Unless otherwise noted, all subsequent quotations from Roethke's poems are taken from this edition, hereafter referred to as "CP."

Roethke conceives of the literary tradition as a "legacy"—"of pain" in the first poem, of property in the second. "The remaining heirs" in "Sale," however, are more vigorous than the "Darling[s] of an infected brood" in the earlier poem; and instead of "blubber[ing] in surprise," they attempt to rid themselves of their legacy by putting it up "For sale." Selling off tradition operates as a metaphor on several levels. It is a wry comment in an almost literal sense on what the poet does when he writes a poem about the past and sends it off to be published; more generally and less literally, it shows Roethke searching for methods by which the modern poet can make use of the past, and the particular way that he discovers in this poem is to dispose of it as if it were old furniture. The present house of poetry, to continue with Roethke's explicit metaphor, is cluttered with the furnishings of our literary ancestors. To prepare for his "open house," Roethke had to throw out the inessential fixtures—the antimacassars, Chippendale chairs, and hand-painted wallpaper. His wish for a "language strict and pure" in his title poem, combined with the sentiments in "Sale," suggest that he wanted to associate himself with a tradition that was likewise "strict and pure"—that he would select—in effect, create—his own tradition, discarding what was worthless, to provide himself with the proper milieu for the creation of his poetry.

Both Roethke's attitude towards the past and some of his images that embody this attitude are reminiscent of Chapter XII in Hawthorne's *The House of the Seven Gables*, also about an inheritance and the relation of the present generation to the preceding ones. Holgrave speaks "of the influence of the Past": " 'Shall we never, never get rid of this Past!' cried he. . . . 'It lies upon the Present like a giant's dead body! In fact, the case is just as if a young giant were compelled to waste all his strength in carrying about the corpse of the old giant, his grandfather, who died a long while ago, and only needs to be decently buried. . . . Whatever we seek to do, of our own free motion, a Dead Man's icy hand obstructs us!' "[3] The image in "Sale" of "grandfather's sinister hovering hand" is expressive of the same heavy oppression of the present by the past suggested in Hawthorne's lines. But just as Holgrave's concept of the past alters in the course of the novel, Roethke's attitudes towards the past change in the course of his career: "I remember the late John Peale Bishop, that fine neglected poet, reading this ['Feud'] and saying, 'You're impassioned, but wrong. The dead can help us.' And he was right; but it took me some years to learn that."[4]

Since Roethke wished to write in a "language strict and pure," "naked" and "spare," he had to exclude certain kinds of diction from his poetry. "I am trying to avoid the sentimental and literary diction of the Georgians or the earlier *Floral Offerings* of the nineteenth century," he wrote in a letter in 1945, "and write a natural sensuous poetry with some symbolical reference in the more complex pieces."[5] His lyric "On the Road to Woodlawn" is closely connected with this passage. The poem is, on one level, about "sentimental and literary diction," an interpretation strengthened by Roethke's using in the verse exactly the same phrase as in the letter—"floral offerings." Two opposing attitudes towards this type of poetry are presented in the poem. One attitude is the same as that stated in the letter: sentimental poetry is dead, and, to use Hawthorne's words again, "needs to be decently buried." "On the Road to Woodlawn" is its funeral. The modern poet should not look to such flaccid verse for his own creations, but should exclude it from his tradition.

Running counter to the decision to inter this poetry, however, is Roethke's nostalgic attachment to it. His poem begins,

[3] Nathaniel Hawthorne, *The House of the Seven Gables*, ed. Hyatt H. Waggoner (Boston: Houghton Mifflin, 1964), p. 158.

[4] "On 'Identity,'" p. 23.

[5] *Selected Letters of Theodore Roethke*, ed. Ralph J. Mills, Jr. (Seattle: University of Washington Press, 1968), p. 113.

I miss the polished brass, the powerful black
 horses,
The drivers creaking the seats of the baroque
 hearses,
The high-piled floral offerings with sentimental
 verses,
The carriages reeking with varnish and stale
 perfume.

(CP 22)

Though the poet has to expel this kind of verse from his working tradition, he regrets its absence and realizes that there yet remains some life in it: "—And the eyes, still vivid, looking up from a sunken room." Indeed, the poem itself shows that a certain amount of vitality subsists; for in the act of consigning this body of poetry to the grave, Roethke used the very kinds of ornate images and Latinate constructions associated with it. The way he finally turned to account this stale sentimental verse was to write about it *qua* sentimental verse—just as in "Sale" and "The Auction," where the dead weight of tradition inhibiting his ability to write was made the subject of his poems and thereby became a provisional solution to the modern poet's abiding problems of what to write about and what to do with the past.

Following "Open House" are several poems about the inability to write. In "Death Piece," the mind is without movement:

Invention sleeps within a skull
No longer quick with light,
The hive that hummed in every cell
Is now sealed honey-tight.

His thought is tied, the curving prow
Of motion moored to rock;
And minutes burst upon a brow
Insentient to shock.

(CP 4)

Instead of the doors of creativity being "widely swung" as in "Open House," they are shut tight. "Interlude" also portrays the poet's failure to create—this time through the image of a dry storm, similar to T. S. Eliot's "dry sterile thunder without rain."[6] The poet "waited for the first rain in the eaves," but

> The rain stayed in its cloud; full
> dark came near;
> The wind lay motionless in the long
> grass.
> The veins within our hands betrayed
> our fear.
> What we had hoped for had not come
> to pass.
>
> (CP 6)

Just as weather vanes show the condition of the atmosphere, so the veins in the hands show the condition of the man. The storm, instead of producing rain, produces chaos, like the "rage" that produces only "witless agony" instead of poetry in "Open House." "The Adamant" continues to develop the theme of the inability to write. "The deed will speak the truth," Roethke declared optimistically in his title poem; but "The Adamant" demonstrates the difficulty of getting at that truth. "Truth never is undone" means not only that truth is invulnerable to attack, but also that it is impossible to reach and release. The poet, trying to get at the core of truth and break it into words, cannot reach it, even using all of the powers of the mind: "Thought does not crush to stone." The truth "lies sealed," just as poetic "invention" remains "sealed honey-tight" in "Death Piece."

"Mid-Country Blow," which follows "The Adamant," presents a way out of the inability to create:

[6] From "The Waste Land," *Collected Poems 1909-1962* (New York: Harcourt, Brace & World, 1963), p. 66. All subsequent quotations from Eliot's poetry are taken from this edition.

All night and all day the wind roared
in the trees,
Until I could think there were waves
rolling high as my bedroom floor;
When I stood at the window, an elm
bough swept to my knees;
The blue spruce lashed like a surf
at the door.

The second dawn I would not have
believed:
The oak stood with each leaf stiff
as a bell.
When I looked at the altered scene,
my eye was undeceived,
But my ear still kept the sound of
the sea like a shell.

(CP 12)

Like Wordsworth's "The Solitary Reaper," this poem is concerned with the function of memory in the creation of poetry. The first stanza describes what was experienced—a storm reminding the speaker of a flood. The wind, which "lay motionless in the long grass" in "Interlude," now roars in the trees; the waves roll, and the spruce lashes like a surf. The entire experience is identified with movement and creativity. The second stanza describes the silent dawn and can be compared with those poems of rigidity and inactivity where the poet was aware of his inability to produce. But here Roethke's memory of personal experience transports him back to a time of motion and productivity.

The memory of the wind provides images of energy for "Mid-Country Blow," but the literary as well as the personal memory may stimulate and provide a model for poetic expression. A case in point is the brief and exquisite lyric "No Bird." C. W. Truesdale, in his article on "Theodore Roethke and the Landscape of American Poetry," writes that this poem, "as William Meredith suggests about many poems in

Open House, might have been written by any gifted and astute imitator of classical English verse."[7] Well, maybe. Except, and this is a most important exception, Roethke did not imitate classical English verse. In fact, he almost never modeled his poems after the general style of any literary period or tradition; instead, he imitated the distinctive practice of individual authors. Truesdale does go on to suggest a specific poet who he thinks may have influenced Roethke's lyric: " 'No Bird,' though a lovely and accomplished epitaph, is Roethke wearing for a moment the mask of Herrick." But Roethke tells us in his title poem "Myself is what I wear," and when he deliberately suggests the cadences and construction of another poet, he has a purpose in doing so. There would be no justification for referring to Herrick's style in "No Bird": there is, I would suggest, a significant reason for echoing the techniques of Emily Dickinson—Roethke wrote the poem as a tribute to the dead poetess. "No Bird" is Emily Dickinson's epitaph. She had once written, "I many times thought Peace had come/When Peace was far away."[8] Hence Roethke begins his poem

Now here is peace for one who knew
The secret heart of sound.
The ear so delicate and true
Is pressed to noiseless ground.
(CP 17)

Roethke explicitly (though subtly) commends the musical tones of Dickinson's poetry, and he pays homage to it implicitly by adopting some of her characteristic practices. He borrows her diction and one of her most frequently

[7] C. W. Truesdale, "Theodore Roethke and the Landscape of American Poetry," *The Minnesota Review*, No. 8 (1968), p. 346. The William Meredith article referred to by Truesdale is "A Steady Storm of Correspondences: Theodore Roethke's Long Journey Out of the Self," in *Theodore Roethke: Essays on the Poetry*, ed. Stein, pp. 36-53.

[8] *The Complete Poems of Emily Dickinson*, ed. Thomas H. Johnson (Boston: Little, Brown and Company, 1957), p. 362. All subsequent quotations from Emily Dickinson are from this edition.

used rhythm patterns, common meter (alternately eight and six syllables to the line), often rhyming abab. Roethke's indebtedness to Emily Dickinson is strikingly revealed by comparing the last stanza of "No Bird" with the last stanza of "On this long storm the Rainbow rose":

> Slow swings the breeze above her head,
> The grasses whitely stir;
> But in this forest of the dead
> No bird awakens her.
>
> ("No Bird")

> The quiet nonchalance of death—
> No Daybreak—can bestir—
> The slow—Archangel's syllables
> Must awaken her!
>
> ("On this long storm . . .")

Moreover, the phrase "forest of the dead" in Roethke's poem is taken from Emily Dickinson's "Our journey had advanced":

> Our pace took sudden awe—
> Our feet—reluctant—led—
> Before—were Cities—but Between—
> The Forest of the Dead—

Since Emily Dickinson was writing about death in both "On this long storm the Rainbow rose" and "Our journey had advanced," it is apt that Roethke summoned up these poems when he composed her epitaph. Although no bird awakens the dead poetess, Roethke's imagination is "awakened" by her poems. Emily Dickinson herself would not have created a poem in this way. She once wrote in a letter to her "Preceptor," Thomas Wentworth Higginson, "I marked a line in One Verse—because I met it after I made it—and never consciously touch a paint, mixed by another person."[9] Roethke borrowed an ample supply of "paint"

[9] *Emily Dickinson's Selected Letters*, ed. Thomas H. Johnson (Cambridge, Massachusetts: Harvard University Press, 1971), p. 179.

from other poets and blended it with his own—until all of his poetry was colored and shaded by his reading. Sometimes, as he himself was well aware, a true poem was not created but was instead "reeking with varnish," like those carriages in "On the Road to Woodlawn"; however, he did not consider his method any less legitimate or creative than that employed by poets whom we often think of as more inventive. One could even define his method with a phrase from Emily Dickinson—"instinct picking up the Key Dropped by Memory."

It is not enough, then, just to place one of Roethke's poems in a tradition; we must find the particular author and even the particular work that the modern poet is responding to. Once the special context is discovered, our entire conception of "No Bird" is irrevocably altered. Indeed, we realize the poem's true subject. In *Theodore Roethke: An Introduction to the Poetry*, Karl Malkoff states that another poem, "The Adamant," belongs "in the metaphysical tradition."[10] Yes, in a vague sense, but again the definite context must be provided to move from Malkoff's loose stylistic label towards Roethke's real interests. Read aloud the following two stanzas from Emily Dickinson's " 'Twas warm—at first—like Us—" and then "The Adamant":

> The Forehead copied Stone—
> The Fingers grew too cold
> To ache—and like a Skater's Brook—
> The busy eyes—congealed—. . . .
>
> And even when with Cords—
> 'Twas lowered, like a Weight—
> It made no Signal, nor demurred,
> But dropped like Adamant.
>
> (" 'Twas warm . . .")

[10] Karl Malkoff, *Theodore Roethke: An Introduction to the Poetry* (New York: Columbia University Press, 1966), p. 36.

Thought does not crush to stone.
The great sledge drops in vain.
Truth never is undone;
Its shafts remain.

The teeth of knitted gears
Turn slowly through the night,
But the true substance bears
The hammer's weight.

Compression cannot break
A center so congealed;
The tool can chip no flake:
The core lies sealed.
("The Adamant")

Roethke is writing a poem about truth. But seeing Emily Dickinson's powerful poem about death from which "The Adamant" descended alters our conception of the tone of his poem. The relationship in Roethke's poem between the speaker and "truth" is, as I have pointed out earlier, one associated with inactivity. Knowing the source underscores the stasis suggested by the poem.

The question here is whether or not Roethke is consciously following Emily Dickinson. In the case of "No Bird," where the poem is so clearly about the poet from whom he is borrowing, it is undoubtedly a process of which he is aware—that he, in fact, designs. With "The Adamant," however, as with so many of Roethke's poems, the relationship between the poet and his sources does not allow us to determine whether or not the course is conscious. Words and images were stored in what Roethke called his "elephantine memory,"[11] and when they took the form of his poem, he may not have been aware of where he first met them or indeed that he had met them anywhere before except in his own mind. Finally, for the reader, the classifications of "conscious" or "unconscious" are not the central issue: the

[11] *Selected Letters*, p. 102.

point is that it happens, time after time. Roethke makes use of a tradition not just in some general sense, but through a unique borrowing of particular portions from other poems.

One of Roethke's early lyrics begins with the end of Gerard Manley Hopkins' "Inversnaid." Hopkins' poem, describing a dark, turbulent stream and its surroundings, concludes with a question and an entreaty:

> What would the world be, once bereft
> Of wet and of wildness? Let them be left,
> O let them be left, wildness and wet;
> Long live the weeds and the wilderness yet.[12]

Roethke chose " 'Long Live the Weeds' " as the title for his poem in which he, like Hopkins, finds value in "the ugly of the universe." It is, writes Roethke, "The rough, the wicked, and the wild/That keep the spirit undefiled":

> With these I match my little wit
> And earn the right to stand or sit,
> Hope, love, create, or drink and die:
> These shape the creature that is I.
> (CP 18)

Roethke must contend with harsh reality and with those earlier poets—in this instance, Hopkins—who wrote about it. Both personal and literary experience "shape the creature that is I." These two types of experience are grasped simultaneously by Roethke's "wit."

The statements about "the rough" and "the wild" can also be read as statements about the language of poetry. Since in "Open House" Roethke called for a "language strict and pure" and in "On the Road to Woodlawn" suggested that he would exclude certain kinds of diction from his poetry, the reader might think that he is going to have a limited range of diction and a rigid concept of decorum to guide him in the choice of his language. But in " 'Long

[12] *Poems of Gerard Manley Hopkins*, ed. W. H. Gardner and N. H. Mackenzie (London: Oxford University Press, 1967), p. 89.

Live the Weeds' " Roethke celebrates a diction that, like the weeds and what they represent in the poem, is unrestricted. The weeds will be kept in his poetry; only the "floral offerings" will be uprooted. The unrestrained approach to language that Roethke commends here is exactly that most thoroughly exemplified in the poetry of Hopkins, who, as poet-critic Donald Davie wrote, "could have found a place for every word in the language if only he could have written enough poems."[13]

After praising Hopkins' diction, Roethke actually imitated, or, as he claimed in a letter to Louise Bogan in 1939, "assimilated" it. The resulting poem, entitled "Praise," is not reprinted in any of his collected works. The letter to Miss Bogan, signed "Theodore Flopkins-Hopkins Roethke," is far more interesting than the poem and contains one of Roethke's attitudes towards past poets: "And what is an ancestor for anyway? (Ans. To assimilate, not to imitate. . . . Thought I had assimilated, etc.)"[14]

One way in which a poet can increase the density and range of meaning in a poem is to borrow a well-known image from another poet, since that single image will bring into his poem some of the meanings and attendant associations it had in the original work. Roethke's "The Premonition" is an almost purely descriptive poem, but if the reader is aware of the source of the appropriated image, then he can read the poem in terms of the themes and context brought in by that source:

> Walking this field I remember
> Days of another summer.
> Oh that was long ago! I kept
> Close to the heels of my father,
> Matching his stride with half-steps
> Until we came to a river.

[13] Donald Davie, *Purity of Diction in English Verse* (London: Routledge & Kegan Paul, 1952), p. 5.

[14] *Selected Letters*, p. 81.

He dipped his hand in the shallow:
Water ran over and under
Hair on a narrow wrist bone;
His image kept following after,—
Flashed with the sun in the ripple.
But when he stood up, that face
Was lost in a maze of water.
(CP 6)

The image of "Hair on a narrow wrist bone" immediately recalls John Donne's "A bracelet of bright haire about the bone" ("The Relique") and "That subtile wreath of haire, which crowns mine arme" ("The Funerall").[15] Therefore, when Roethke writes, "His image kept following after," he refers to the visual image (the impression of the father produced by the reflection from the water), the image in the mind (the picture of the father as produced by the son's memory), and the poetic image (the figure of speech taken from Donne). Once the reader realizes that Donne's poems about mortality are the source and context of the adopted image, he understands that "the premonition" referred to is of death. To enlarge the meaning of his poem, Roethke relied not only upon his own awareness of a literary tradition, but also upon the reader's awareness of this tradition.

Many of the early poems are virtuoso pieces in which Roethke strove to improve his technical skills by constantly imitating his competitors, living and dead. The model for "This Light,"[16] as he stated in his article "How to Write Like Somebody Else," was Elinor Wylie:

"Now I didn't clutch a copy of Wylie in one hand, and write the piece with the other. Actually, I had been reading a lot of Vaughan, and a friend of mine suggested I do a poem

[15] John Donne, *The Elegies and the Songs and Sonnets*, ed. Helen Gardner (Oxford: Clarendon Press, 1965), pp. 89-90. All subsequent quotations from Donne are from this edition.

[16] "This Light" appeared in *American Poetry Journal*, 17 (November, 1934), 3, and in John Holmes, *The Poet's Work* (New York, 1939), pp. 132-133.

on 'Light.' I took—I suppose from Wylie—the devices of metaphor on a string—as in her piece

> This sorrow was small and vulnerable and
> shortlived;
> It was neither earth nor stone . . .

which itself derives, I believe, from Shelley."[17]

Roethke went beyond merely responding to a single poet and actually formed a tradition of poets, linked together in this instance by similar themes and techniques and in all cases by their usefulness to him as a practising poet. In this same article he described W. H. Auden as "a real magpie, with a cormorant's rapacity and the long memory of the elephant," who "pillages the past . . . or the present," and who snatched some of the phrases for his ballad "As I Walked Out One Evening" from Robert Graves's "Full Moon."[18] Roethke, however, does not acknowledge his indebtedness to Auden for many of the elements in his "Ballad of the Clairvoyant Widow"; yet for this poem he pillaged much more from Auden than Auden did from Graves. Thus Roethke's early poems show how ideas and techniques are communicated from one poet to another, forming a tradition or community of poets—in "This Light," Vaughan, Shelley, Wylie, and Roethke, and in "The Ballad of the Clairvoyant Widow," Graves, Auden, and Roethke.

"The Buds Now Stretch"[19] was overtly based upon the rhythms and vocabulary of Leonie Adams. In fact, Roethke once told Miss Adams that it was "one of the finest poems" she had ever written.[20] He writes more seriously and at greater length about this poem in his essay on imitation, suggesting that the past is more than just a collection of

[17] From "How to Write Like Somebody Else," *On the Poet and His Craft*, p. 64.

[18] "How to Write Like Somebody Else," p. 67.

[19] "The Buds Now Stretch" appeared in *Adelphi*, No. 6 (April, 1933) and in *The New York Times*, Vol. 88 (November 9, 1938), p. 22. This poem is not included in *The Collected Poems*.

[20] *Selected Letters*, p. 213.

patterns to be imitated and that writing in response to other poets is not a restriction of one's own abilities, but a method of realizing those abilities:

"I hate to abandon that poem: I feel it's something Miss Adams and I have created: a literary lovechild. Put it this way: I loved her so much, her poetry, that I just *had* to become, for a brief moment, a part of her world. For it *is* her world, and I had filled myself with it, and I *had* to create something that would honor her in her own terms. That, I think, expresses as best I can what really goes on with the hero- or heroine-worshiping young. I didn't cabbage those effects in cold blood; that poem is a true release in its way. I was too clumsy and stupid to articulate my own emotions: she helped me to say something about the external world, helped me convince myself that maybe, if I kept at it, eventually I might write a poem of my own, with the accent on my own speech [Roethke's emphasis]."[21]

Compare T. S. Eliot's remarks from "The Music of Poetry":

"It is not from rules, or by cold-blooded imitation of style, that we learn to write: we learn by imitation indeed, but by a deeper imitation than is achieved by analysis of style. When we imitated Shelley, it was not so much from a desire to write as he did, as from an invasion of the adolescent self by Shelley, which made Shelley's way, for the time, the only way in which to write."[22]

Not only did Roethke adopt the theories and even some of the phrases of Eliot's essay (most noticeably the "cold blood"), but, more importantly, he demonstrated in his poems, such as "The Buds Now Stretch," the veracity of Eliot's comments on how young poets learn their craft.

"The only way to learn to manipulate any kind of English verse," Eliot wrote, "[is] by assimilation and imitation, by becoming so engrossed in the work of a particular poet that

[21] "How to Write Like Somebody Else," p. 66.

[22] T. S. Eliot, "The Music of Poetry," *On Poetry and Poets* (New York: Farrar, Straus & Cudahy, 1957), p. 19.

one could produce a recognizable derivative."[23] Roethke repeated and extended Eliot's ideas:

"Imitation, conscious imitation, is one of the great methods, perhaps *the* method of learning to write. The ancients, the Elizabethans, knew this, profited by it, and were not disturbed. As a son of Ben, Herrick more than once rewrote Jonson, who, in turn, drew heavily on the classics. And so on. The poems are not less good for this: the final triumph is what the language does, not what the poet can do, or display. The poet's ultimate loyalty—the phrase belongs to Stanley Kunitz—is to the poem. The language itself is a compound, or, to change the figure, a bitch. The paradoxical thing, as R. P. Blackmur said of some of the young in the 'thirties, is that the most original poets are the most imitative. The remark is profound: if a writer has something to say, it will come through. The very fact he has the support of a tradition, or an older writer, will enable him to be more himself—or more than himself.

"In a time when the romantic notion of the inspired poet still has considerable credence, true 'imitation' takes a certain courage. One dares to stand up to a great style, to compete with papa."[24]

Roethke suggests that the modern poet should move away from the Romantic concept of personal expression and return to the arts of imitation in order to become a part of a tradition and thereby overcome his own limitations. He must, in effect, march through the history of poetry—rewrite the poems of the past—that he may come out at the end of his journey a poet who has absorbed the tradition and who thus may take one step forward and add to that tradition. Roethke's ideas here are similar to Eliot's conception of "an escape from personality" in his essay on "Tradition and the Individual Talent." "No poet, no artist of any art," Eliot wrote, "has his complete meaning alone. His significance, his appreciation is the appreciation of his relation

23 "The Music of Poetry," p. 18.

24 "How to Write Like Somebody Else," pp. 69-70.

to the dead poets and artists. You cannot value him alone; you must set him, for contrast and comparison, among the dead. I mean this as a principle of aesthetic, not merely historical, criticism."[25] Eliot and Roethke were interested in tradition not primarily as literary historians, but as practicing poets. Roethke, instead of waiting for the critic to make evaluative comparisons, placed himself "among the dead" and the living poets to direct us to measure his achievement against theirs.

In this first volume, however, the standard for judgment is none too high. Instead of really trying "to compete with papa," Roethke settled for vying mainly with some of the better poetesses—Emily Dickinson, Elinor Wylie, and Leonie Adams. This is not to suggest that they are not good poets, but only that they do not provide the substantial tradition through which the young poet can move from mimicry to assimilation. Dickinson is a poet of the first rank, but in the hands of another, her singular style can become a verbal trick keeping the poet from his own voice rather than leading him to it. At times Roethke is uncomfortably close to his own description of a "poetaster" "whose mama pays the bills!" (CP 24). Although his title poem states

> My heart keeps open house,
> My doors are widely swung,

in his earliest poems he, quite conversely, selected his own society, then shut the door. It was not until later volumes that he matched himself against and adopted for his own purposes the poetry of major British and American writers.

[25] T. S. Eliot, "Tradition and the Individual Talent," *Selected Essays*, pp. 4-5.

II

Sympathetic Imitation

"At a time like ours . . . ," T. S. Eliot has written, "we are inclined . . . to exaggerate the importance of the innovators at the expense of the reputation of the developers."[1] Nearly all of the critics who reviewed *Open House* agreed that the lyrics were highly traditional, though few attempted to define the tradition; but because of the revolutionary appearance of some of the poems in *The Lost Son*, the critics allowed their enthusiasm over Roethke's innovations to obscure their judgments of his developments within a tradition.[2] One of the most ignored yet most important components of the tradition that Roethke in effect created for himself is the poetry of William Wordsworth. When writing the *Lost Son* poems, Roethke repeatedly turned to Wordsworth, particularly to Book I of *The Prelude*, as a source for titles, images, and ideas. John Wain, one of the few critics to discover even a coincidental link between Roethke and Wordsworth, writes that "the greenhouse occupies the same place in Roethke's poetic evolution as the hills and dales of the Lake District do in Wordsworth's."[3] But the relationship goes deeper still: close attention to underlying parallels between Roethke and Wordsworth can reveal that Wordsworth's poems written about the hills and dales of the Lake District helped Roethke to develop the appropriate language for his own poems on man's response

[1] T. S. Eliot, *On Poetry and Poets*, pp. 28-29.

[2] See, for example, Joseph Bennett, "Recent Verse," *Hudson Review*, No. 7 (Summer, 1954), p. 305. In the long poems, Bennett writes, Roethke's "is an individualism operating in disregard of the canons of traditional verse."

[3] John Wain, "The Monocle of My Sea-Faced Uncle," *Theodore Roethke: Essays on the Poetry*, ed. Stein, p. 61.

to nature. Literary memory complements and guides personal memory in the creation of Roethke's poetry.

From Roethke's imitations and intimations we can also discover an implicit criticism of Wordsworth's poetry. In several significant ways, this critique of the Romantic poet anticipates some of the best recent Wordsworth scholarship, written twenty years after Roethke's Wordsworthian poems. My purpose in quoting from Geoffrey H. Hartman and Herbert Lindenberger is to show not only how close Roethke is to Wordsworth, but also how close Roethke's conception of Wordsworth is to the viewpoint of these two modern Wordsworth scholars.

One of the clearest examples of the connection between the poets is the similar themes, structures, and images linking Roethke's "Moss-Gathering" with Wordsworth's "Nutting." Both poets, writing in the first person, describe a distinct, private event in their boyhoods. The arrangement of the episodes is the same: the child goes alone into the woods to gather some plant, destroys "the natural order of things," and suffers for his act of destruction. These two brief lyrics follow the traditional tragic rhythm of action—purpose, passion, and perception—as described by Kenneth Burke and Francis Fergusson. Another pattern even more particularly evident in these two poems is the "heroic pattern of quest, ravage, spirit-vengeance" described by Geoffrey H. Hartman in *Wordsworth's Poetry 1787-1814*.[4] Hartman further suggests that the bower described by Wordsworth is the bower of Renaissance Romance. He quotes from Wordsworth's prefatory essay to *The Borderers* to suggest that "the youngster [in 'Nutting'] is not unlike 'the Orlando of Ariosto, the Cardenio of Cervantes, who lays waste the groves that would shelter him.'" Or, I would suggest, the child who destroys the bower "with . . . merciless ravage" is also like Guyon in Book II, Canto XII of the *Faerie Queene*, who overthrows "the Bowre of Blisse" "with rigour pit-

[4] Geoffrey H. Hartman, *Wordsworth's Poetry 1787-1814* (New Haven: Yale University Press, 1964), p. 74.

tilesse." The bower is a metaphor for the heroic kind of poetry associated with authors like Ariosto and Spenser, a poetry in which the interest in the heroic human energies takes precedence over the emotions of the human heart and the community of feeling between man and nature. In "Nutting," Wordsworth reaches out for a new conception of imagination and of Romantic poetry based on the sympathetic feelings in man, rather than on his heroic powers.

Just as Wordsworth's poem makes use of the tradition of certain Renaissance Romances, Roethke in "Moss-Gathering" turns back to "Nutting" to sharpen and substantiate his sense of these patterns. For both Wordsworth and Roethke, the experience described is above all instructive: it leads to an apprehension of nature as it is implicated in human feelings. The educative process can begin only after the heroes leave home to begin their quest. Wordsworth writes, "I left our cottage-threshold, sallying forth."[5] The boy steps upon the threshold of manhood and of consciousness to enter "some far-distant wood. . . ."

> O'er path-less rocks,
> Through beds of matted fern, and tangled thickets,
> Forcing my way.
>
> (14-16)

All of the poems preceding "Moss-Gathering" in *The Lost Son* take place in or close to the greenhouse. But in this poem the child leaves the greenhouse, which Roethke sometimes refers to as his symbol for a womb, and enters "that swampland." The protagonists journey to similar places: Wordsworth describes the nook he comes to as a "green and mossy bower," where he sees "green stones . . . fleeced with moss, under the shady trees"; Roethke describes the "dark-green" moss, "those carpets of green," and "the spongy yellowish moss of the marshes."

[5] *The Poetical Works of William Wordsworth*, ed. E. de Selincourt, second edition (Oxford: Clarendon Press, 1952), II, 211. All further quotations from Wordsworth's poems, except for *The Prelude*, are from this edition.

Following the description of the calm landscape is its devastation. Wordsworth writes,

> Then up I rose,
> And dragged to earth both branch and bough, with crash
> And merciless ravage: and the shady nook
> Of hazels, and the green and mossy bower,
> Deformed and sullied, patiently gave up
> Their quiet being.
>
> (43-48)

Roethke writes,

> I dug loose those carpets
> Of green, or plunged to my elbows in the spongy yellowish moss of the marshes:
> . . . pulling off flesh from the living planet.
>
> (CP 40)

The protagonists force their violence upon a passive and suffering nature. In both passages there are suggestions of sexual plunder. Early in his poem, Wordsworth describes the "dear nook" as "a virgin scene":

> A little while I stood,
> Breathing with such suppression of the heart
> As joy delights in; and, with wise restraint
> Voluptuous, fearless of rival, eyed
> The banquet.
>
> (21-25)

There is in Roethke's poem as in Wordsworth's a sexual overtone—not, however, as an end in itself, but as one of many means of establishing the energy and depth of emotion to be experienced in "Moss-Gathering." The basic patterns of Roethke's poem do not spring from a disturbed subconscious but rather from the conscious exploitation of his poetic heritage. In *Theodore Roethke: An Introduction to the Poetry*, Karl Malkoff, believing that the "esthetic" of the greenhouse poems is their "rooting in sensuous experience,"[6] is led to the conclusion that "Moss-Gathering" is about masturbation—"pulling off flesh." An "esthetic" of Roethke's poems that grounds them in a union of literary experience with sensuous experience leads us to a less limiting critical perspective on his poetry. The experiences in "Moss-Gathering" may well be rooted deep in Roethke's subconscious mind, but the method by which these private experiences are formed into poetry has as its necessary condition his ability to relate them to patterns he discovers in other poets.

Wordsworth's and Roethke's responses to the experience of destroying the natural order are almost identical: both feel a deep sense of guilt over their actions.

> Ere from the mutilated bower I turned
> Exulting, rich beyond the wealth of kings,
> I felt a sense of pain when I beheld
> The silent trees, and saw the intruding sky.
> ("Nutting," 50-53)

> And afterwards I always felt mean,
> jogging back over the logging road,
> As if I had broken the natural order
> of things in that swampland;
> Disurbed some rhythm, old and of
> vast importance,
> By pulling off flesh from the living
> planet;
> As if I had committed, against the whole
> scheme of life, a desecration.
> ("Moss-Gathering")

[6] Karl Malkoff, p. 50.

At the end of the poems, Wordsworth and Roethke invest nature with qualities of human feeling. Before, unaware of these feelings in nature, they were also unaware of these feelings in themselves. Hartman, in explaining the theme of "Nutting," could just as accurately be explaining the theme of "Moss-Gathering" when he writes that "the subject . . . is not the life in nature, or its secret manifestation, but how the child's willful consciousness matures into the sympathetic imagination."[7] The child destroys his self-centeredness along with the bower.

The incident is for both poets a central experience in the development of their poetic faculties. Wordsworth's experience in "Nutting" leads him to a new awareness of his relationship to and sympathy with nature that generates and "rolls through" the majority of his poems. The experience teaches Roethke not only that nature is pervaded by a spiritual presence but that it is informed with order. It is necessary for Roethke as a poet to have a vision of order, an order in which he can share but which is greater than himself. In the first few poems in *The Lost Son*, he finds an order in the theories of Frazer and Jung and identifies vegetative cycles with human cycles. In "Moss-Gathering," following Wordsworth's "Nutting," he finds another vision of order: the experience with nature illuminates his own feelings and brings him a vision of the rhythms of nature that he can use in his own creations.

Whereas the protagonist of "Moss-Gathering" broke "the natural order of things," in "Old Florist" he aids and supports that order. All of the Florist's energies are expended on, almost into, the plants, so that life and order are bound together: the man who orders the greenhouse gives life. The Old Florist as a unique individual, rather than as a representative type (such as the Gardener in Shakespeare's *Richard II*), is close in characterization to Wordsworth's Solitaries, such as the Old Cumberland Beggar and the Old Leech-

[7] Hartman, p. 75.

gatherer from "Resolution and Independence," who live near to nature and whose worthiness and wisdom are a result of active, direct association with nature. Roethke's Old Florist similarly acquires his strength of character through his intimate relationship with the natural setting in which the poet finds and places him. The Florist and Wordsworth's Solitaries share many basic characteristics. Wordsworth writes of the Old Cumberland Beggar,

> Him from my childhood have I known; and then
> He was so old, he seems not older now.
> ("The Old Cumberland Beggar," 22-23)

Like "this Old Man," the Old Florist gives the appearance of being perpetual. Roethke's use of participles suggests that the florist's actions are always continuing:

> That hump of a man bunching chrysanthemums
> Or pinching-back asters, or planting azaleas,
> Tamping and stamping dirt into pots—

The physical description of the Old Florist as "that hump of a man" relates him with Wordsworth's Old Leechgatherer whose "body was bent double, feet and head/Coming together in life's pilgrimage" ("Resolution and Independence," 66-67). In spite of their physical appearance and low station in life, both figures are invested with great dignity.

The heroism of the Old Florist is characteristic of the heroism of Wordsworth's Michael, a courage not evidenced by bold, energetic deeds, but through the power of enduring. Even after the old shepherd loses his only son to "the dissolute city," he continues:

> Among the rocks
> He went, and still looked up to sun and cloud,
> And listened to the wind; and, as before,
> Performed all kinds of labour for his sheep,
> And for the land . . .
> ("Michael," 455-459)

Similarly the Old Florist, in spite of his advanced age, can still manage his world of plants and can "stand all night watering roses, his feet blue in rubber boots." The Old Florist gives of himself in order to create and preserve the beauty of the roses. He becomes bent and his feet become frozen as he dedicates himself to the maintenance of a beauty and order larger than himself. He in turn receives dignity from his dedication.

Roethke as a child saw the florist in the same way Wordsworth as "a rambling school-boy" saw the shepherd:

> I felt his presence in his own domain,
> As of a lord and master, or a power,
> Or genius, under Nature, under God,
> Presiding.
>
> (*Prelude*, Book VIII, 257-260)[8]

In his poem, Roethke sees the Old Florist as a presiding presence, as "lord and master" of the greenhouse, "his own domain," with the power of life and death: he could

> . . . drown a bug in one spit of tobacco juice,
> Or fan life into wilted sweet-peas with his hat.

By using "fan life into" rather than the expected phrase "fan into life," Roethke emphasizes this god-like power of the florist. It would be impossible to claim here that Wordsworth's poems are the immediate source for Roethke's poem, but a comparison of Roethke's "Old Florist" and Wordsworth's Solitaries shows that Roethke is clearly working in that poetic tradition in which Wordsworth is central.

As a source for his brief lyric "Child on Top of a Greenhouse," Roethke again turns to Wordsworth. Compare Roethke's poem with a section from Book I of *The Prelude.*

[8] William Wordsworth, *The Prelude*, ed. E. de Selincourt, second edition (Oxford: Clarendon Press, 1959), p. 285. All subsequent quotations from *The Prelude* are taken from this edition and are from the 1850 version unless otherwise noted.

Child on Top of a Greenhouse

The wind billowing out the seat of my britches,
My feet crackling splinters of glass and dried putty,
The half-grown chrysanthemums staring up
 like accusers,
Up through the streaked glass, flashing with sunlight,
A few white clouds all rushing eastward.
A line of elms plunging and tossing like horses,
And everyone, everyone pointing up and shouting!
(CP 43)

The heart is almost mine with which I felt,
From some hill-top on sunny afternoons,
The paper kite high among fleecy clouds
Pull at her rein like an impetuous courser;
Or, from the meadows sent on gusty days,
Beheld her breast the wind, then suddenly
Dashed headlong, and rejected by the storm.
(*Prelude*, Childhood and Schooltime,
Book I, 492-498)

Both poems are poems of recollection.[9] Wordsworth and Roethke present a description of the childhood mind, although we are constantly aware that it is the adult mind remembering the experience. The joy is active and exuberant. The child is king of the mountain: he is on top of his world, a hill for Wordsworth, the greenhouse for Roethke. Wind, sunlight, and clouds are in both poems the natural companions for the child's exuberance. The two poets use the image of a spirited horse to convey a feeling of impulsive, rushing joy.

Through the acts of nutting and moss-gathering, Words-

[9] The children were five at the time of the events. Wordsworth describes himself in Book I, line 288, of *The Prelude* as "a five years' child." Roethke at one point titled his poem "Adventure at Five." Theodore Roethke Collection, University of Washington, Seattle (Literary Manuscripts Poetry. Box 18, A-C).

worth and Roethke violated natural order; through the act of stealing, Wordsworth in Book I of the *Prelude* violates not natural order but the order of man's society. Yet it is nature and not man who accuses him of his transgressing, as in the woodcock snaring and boat-stealing episodes (317-325, 373-385). Roethke in "Child on Top of a Greenhouse" also invests nature with moral qualities that we normally associate with human beings: "the half-grown chrysanthemums staring up like accusers." The child, by climbing on top of the glass house, has disobeyed his parents—has broken the laws of his immediate society—but it is "half-grown chrysanthemums," not adults, who he feels blame him. Roethke repeats in his poem the same conceptions of nature moralized found in Wordsworth's two stealing episodes.

Roethke's habits of mind as a poet seem to be focused on the discovery of specific lines and particular poems that he could use for his own purposes. He is not, like some of our best literary critics, interested in general and philosophical concepts of tradition and milieu. In a telling essay Roethke wrote as a student on "the problem of the affinities between Vaughan and Wordsworth," his interest is in "the close parallel between language." His examples are "shined in my angel infancy" (Vaughan) and "Heaven lies about us in our infancy" (Wordsworth)—also "And in those weaker glories spy—shadows of eternity" (Vaughan) and "But trailing clouds of glory" and "those shadowy recollections" (Wordsworth). Roethke further writes, "It is perhaps not without significance that many words which students will recognize as 'Wordsworthian' occur frequently in Vaughan. To mention only a few at random: *calm*, *pure*, *serene*, *mansion*, *streams*, *shine*, *privacy*, *secret*, *ring*, *white*."[10] Of course it is proper, indeed enlightening, for us to consider Roethke's position within a tradition in a general, even

[10] Theodore Roethke Collection, University of Washington, Seattle (Theodore Roethke as Student. Box 60, Folders 12 and 13). Roethke did not see that Vaughan and Wordsworth are working from a common source—the Psalms.

philosophical, sense. But as a practicing poet, Roethke's first concern was with the specifics of words, lines, and rhythms.

Roethke follows "Child on Top of a Greenhouse" with "Flower Dump" and then ends Part I of *The Lost Son* with "Carnations":

> Pale blossoms, each balanced on a single
> jointed stem,
> The leaves curled back in elaborate Corinthian
> scrolls;
> And the air cool, as if drifting down from
> wet hemlocks,
> Or rising out of ferns not far from water,
> A crisp hyacinthine coolness,
> Like that clear autumnal weather of eternity,
> The windless perpetual morning above a
> September cloud.
>
> (CP 43)

The word "carnation" comes from the Latin *carnatio*, meaning "fleshiness." But Roethke's carnations are not these deep red, fleshy flowers: they are "pale blossoms" (in fact he originally described them as "pale souls") with their "leaves curled back in elaborate Corinthian scrolls." Roethke connects the ephemeral flower with the highly wrought art of an ancient culture, thus imaging the mutable flower as a permanent artifact. His process is contained in his use of the word "hyacinthine": the hyacinth is both a gem and a flower. Roethke's method was again influenced by Wordsworth. Compare, for example, his "perpetual morning" with Wordsworth's "perpetual dawn" ("Epistle to Sir George Beaumont") or "Carnations" with the following passage from Book I of the *Prelude*:

> Yes, I remember when the changeful earth
> And twice five summers on my mind had stamped
> The faces of the moving year, even then
> I held unconscious intercourse with beauty

Old as creation, drinking in a pure
Organic pleasure from the silver wreaths
Of curling mist, or from the level plain
Of waters coloured by impending clouds.
(559-566)

The verbal echoes are not as strong as they are in some cases (although the same three words—"curl," "water," and "cloud"—are used in both passages and in precisely the same order), but Wordsworth's basic conception of nature in this passage is quite likely the inspiration for Roethke's handling of the same theme. Wordsworth, like Roethke in "Carnations," is writing about beauty's quality of immortality. He holds "intercourse with beauty": there is an interchange between them. From beauty Wordsworth derives "a pure organic pleasure"; to beauty in return he gives permanence. He images the "curling mist" as "silver wreaths," thereby causing the insubstantial and almost imperceptible mist to have form and density.

Through the interchange of the impermanence of nature for the permanence of art, Wordsworth and Roethke hold "intercourse with beauty." Just as the two poets unite art and nature, they unite past and present, unconsciousness and consciousness. As observers of natural beauty in childhood, they were not conceptually aware of the process they were involved in as they are when they write their poems about this process. As "Child on Top of a Greenhouse" and "Carnations" illustrate, there is a complex interrelationship between Roethke's non-linguistic experiences in his childhood and similar experiences he finds in poetry. He brings together in a unique unity a combination of his personal experience and his experience of literature, making his poems an act of both creation and discovery.

Many of the metaphors basic to the greenhouse poems are rooted in Wordsworth. In the process of transplanting them from Wordsworth's poetry into his own, Roethke makes some subtle changes. Wordsworth's "Fair seed-time had my soul" (*Prelude*, Book I, 301) is the metaphor that forms the basis for many of *The Lost Son* poems. Roethke takes "seed-time" in both a figurative and a literal sense; he then expands the literal meaning of Wordsworth's line, while at the same time reducing the general concept of seed-time to a specific perspective on the actual process of a seed sprouting, as in the following passage from "Cuttings (*later*)":

> I can hear, underground, that sucking
> and sobbing,
> In my veins, in my bones I feel it,—
> The small waters seeping upward,
> The tight grains parting at last.
> When sprouts break out,
> Slippery as fish,
> I quail, lean to beginnings, sheath-wet.
> (CP 37)

Roethke takes Wordsworth's metaphor literally, and in addition he preserves all its metaphoric significance. He uses a similar method in "The Minimal," moving from Wordsworth's general statements about Nature's "healing pow'r" (*Descriptive Sketches*, 1793, line 14) to particular one-celled microorganisms and concurrently from a purely metaphoric meaning to a literal and metaphoric one:

> I study the lives on a leaf: the little
> Sleepers, numb nudgers in cold dimensions,
> Beetles in caves, newts, stone-deaf fishes,
> Lice tethered to long limp subterranean weeds,
> Squirmers in bogs,
> And bacterial creepers
> Wriggling through wounds
> Like elvers in ponds,
> Their wan mouths kissing the warm sutures,
> Cleaning and caressing,
> Creeping and healing.
> (CP 50)

Wordsworth is concerned with nature's "healing influence that can creep" ("The Unremitting Voice," 10); Roethke, with the individual microscopic mouths of "bacterial creepers . . . healing." Typically, the modern poet concretizes what is only metaphoric in nineteenth-century poetry.

In a context of poems full of the force of nature, "Dolor," a poem about the business world, is notable for its lack of energy. Unlike "Root Cellar," where the "Bulbs broke out of boxes hunting for chinks in the dark" (CP 38), in the "immaculate public places" of "Dolor" the pencils remain "Neat in their boxes." The stiff, decaying "institutions" are devoid of plants; the only thing alive in them is "dust." When Roethke writes a poem about modern desolation and devitalization, he turns to the spokesman of such poetry, T. S. Eliot, for a couple of key phrases which make the reader immediately think of the tedious, enervated world of J. Alfred Prufrock:

> And I have known the eyes already, known
> them all—. . .
> And I have known the arms already, known
> them all—
> ("The Love Song of J. Alfred Prufrock,"
> 55 and 62)

> I have known the inexorable sadness of
> pencils . . .
> ("Dolor," 1)

> I have seen the moment of my greatness
> flicker,
> And I have seen the eternal Footman hold
> my coat, and snicker.
> ("The Love Song of J. Alfred Prufrock,"
> 84-85)

> And I have seen dust from the walls of
> institutions . . .
> ("Dolor," 9)

While the tone of "Dolor" is dominated by Eliot's influence and the title may have been suggested by his lines "talking of trivial things/In ignorance and in knowledge of eternal dolour" ("Ash-Wednesday"), the structure of the poem is quite similar to some of the descriptive passages in Wordsworth's *Prelude*. For Roethke, just as for Wordsworth and many other Romantic poets, there is a disparity between exterior and interior experience, and each has its own mode of expression. Both Wordsworth and Roethke use the city as one of their symbols for the external world and they present this world that is too much with us through enumerating separate items in it:

> Thou endless stream of men and moving things! . . .
> The comers and the goers face to face,
> Face after face; the string of dazzling wares,
> Shop after shop, with symbols, blazon'd names,
> And all the tradesman's honours overhead:
> Here, fronts of houses, like a title-page
> With letters huge inscribed from top to toe.
> (*Prelude*, Book VII, lines 151, 156-161)

> . . . dolor of pad and paper-weight,
> All the misery of manilla folders and mucilage,
> Desolation in immaculate public places,
> Lonely reception room, lavatory, switchboard,
> The unalterable pathos of basin and pitcher,
> Ritual of multigraph, paper-clip, comma,
> Endless duplication of lives and objects.
> ("Dolor," CP 46)

These passages are purposely rigid. Roethke, especially, seems to be writing an annual inventory. There is no reciprocal relationship between the poets and the places. When Wordsworth describes the "endless stream of men and moving things" and Roethke the "endless duplication of lives and objects," they assume the point of view of an observer who feels no communion with these externals.

The central experiences in *The Prelude* and in *The Lost Son*, however, are not outer but inner ones in which the poet at once is in and interacts with nature. Wordsworth uses the word "inner"—as in "inner pulse," "inner heart," and "inner eye"—to distinguish the life of the mind, so important to a poet, from the physical world and the physical senses. He sometimes presents a similar yet different perspective on this inner reality by using the word "under" instead of "inner," as in "under soul," "under-thirst," "under-powers," "under-agents," "under-sense," and "under-presences." Because "under" shows depth as well as position, it operates as an even more energetic image of movement than "inner." Both "inner" and "under" are used by Wordsworth to identify the poet's imaginative faculties with which he can "see into the life of things," rather than to describe actual physical location.[11] Roethke, however, takes the word "under" in a literal sense, placing the point of view of several of the *Lost Son* poems beneath the natural world into whose life and energies he attempts to see. Roethke accepts Wordsworth's metaphoric "under" and transforms it into the actual position of his speaker in "Weed Puller":

Under the concrete benches,
Hacking at black hairy roots,—
Those lewd monkey-tails hanging
    from drainholes,—
Digging into the soft rubble
    underneath,
Webs and weeds,
Grubs and snails and sharp sticks,
Or yanking tough fern-shapes,
Coiled green and thick, like
    dripping smilax,

[11] Many of these concepts about Wordsworth's poetry are explored in greater detail in Herbert Lindenberger's *On Wordsworth's Prelude* (Princeton: Princeton University Press, 1963). See particularly pp. 166-169. Lindenberger, of course, is not concerned with Roethke in this study.

Tugging all day at perverse life:
The indignity of it!—
With everything blooming above me,
Lilies, pale-pink cyclamen, roses,
Whole fields lovely and inviolate,—
Me down in that fetor of weeds,
Crawling on all fours,
Alive, in a slippery grave.

(CP 39)

Roethke quite literally becomes an "under-agent," to use Wordsworth's phrase. Both Wordsworth and Roethke begin their imaginative explorations of nature and their communion with it by focusing our attention on an "inner" or "under" concept of imaginative vision central to their poetry.

Thomas De Quincey in his *Literary Reminiscences* points out a particularly effective use of another spatial description as a metaphor for a psychic state:

And they [the owls] would shout
Across the watry Vale, and shout again,
Responsive to his call, with quivering peals,
And long halloos and screams, and echoes loud
Redoubled and redoubled; concourse wild
Of mirth and jocund din! And when it chanced
That pauses of deep silence mock'd his skill,
Then sometimes, in that silence, while he hung
Listening, a gentle shock of mild surprize
Has carried far into his heart the voice
Of mountain torrents; or the visible scene
Would enter unawares into his mind
With all its solemn imagery, its rocks,
Its woods, and that uncertain Heaven, receiv'd
Into the bosom of the steady Lake.

(1805 version of the *Prelude*, Book v, 374-388)

"This very expression, 'far,' " writes De Quincey, "by which space and its infinities are attributed to the human heart, and to its capacities of re-echoing the sublimities of nature, has always struck me as with a flash of sublime revelation."[12] Similarly, Roethke uses a series of spatial images to describe the workings of his imagination and again, as in Wordsworth, to show the interconnections between a stimulus from the exterior world and the inner life of the poet:

When I saw that clumsy crow
Flap from a wasted tree,
A shape in the mind rose up:
Over the gulfs of dream
Flew a tremendous bird
Further and further away
Into a moonless black,
Deep in the brain, far back.
("Night Crow," CP 49)

Implicit in both Wordsworth's and Roethke's poems is the same concept of the poet's imagination, which is contingent upon a continual communion between the natural world and the mind of the poet. The same imaginative process and some of the same images, as in Roethke's "Night Crow," can be found in Wordsworth's sonnet "Return":

A dark plume fetch me from yon blasted yew,
Perched on whose top the Danish Raven croaks;
Aloft, the imperial Bird of Rome invokes
Departed ages, shedding where he flew
Loose fragments of wild wailing, that bestrew
The clouds and thrill the chambers of the rocks . . .

The crow on the wasted tree and the raven on the blasted yew both suggest a concept of history to the poets. Wordsworth's poem begins with a description of nature that calls up a specific historical period. Roethke deals with human history in an anthropological and psychological sense, rather than in the chronological sense that Wordsworth uses. The process of the imagination is the same in both poems, but

[12] Thomas De Quincey, *Literary Reminiscences*, quoted in Lindenberger, p. 42.

Wordsworth is concerned with the external history of human cultures and Roethke with the internal history of human psychology.

Although these parallels between Roethke and Wordsworth do not in every case point to actual sources, they help the critic to establish the proper ambience in which to place the modern poet. Roethke's comments on his contemporaries suggest that he used this method of comparison to illuminate and evaluate their works. He praises Louise Bogan highly because in her poetry "the ground beat of the great tradition can be heard, with the necessary subtle variations."[13] He hears this "ground beat" in the last stanza of her poem "Come, Break With Time":

> Take the rocks' speed
> And Earth's heavy measure.
> Let buried seed
> Drain out time's pleasure,
> Take time's decrees.
> Come, cruel ease.

"I am reminded, perhaps eccentrically," writes Roethke, "of Wordsworth's

> No motion has she now, no force;
>   She neither hears nor sees;
> Rolled round in earth's diurnal course,
>   With rocks, and stones, and trees.

In this instance, I feel one poem supports, gives additional credence, to the other."[14] For Roethke, Bogan's poem is made better because it can be compared to and implicated in another poem. Roethke is in effect reading her poem by first placing it in a tradition and then seeing it from the perspective of that tradition. Dealing with Roethke's own poems from the perspective of his involvement in a Words-

[13] "The Poetry of Louise Bogan," *On the Poet and His Craft*, p. 148.
[14] "The Poetry of Louise Bogan," p. 139.

worthian tradition also gives "additional credence" to his poetry. Unlike his earlier direct borrowings, for example from Emily Dickinson, Roethke's relationship with Wordsworth is much more than a matter of verbal or even thematic echoes. He felt a sympathetic companionship with Wordsworth's life as well as with his art. In their childhoods both poets had profoundly intense and memorable experiences in nature, and Wordsworth's transmutations of these experiences into poetry (which frequently form the subject of the poems themselves) offered a stimulus and model to Roethke's ambitions as a poet.

In 1951 Doubleday published Roethke's next book of poems, *Praise to the End!* Wordsworth remains a central, unifying influence, for, as Roethke pointed out in a letter to Ralph J. Mills, Jr. ". . . some of those titles in (*Praise to the End!*) are little quotes from those I think of as ancestors. 'Praise to the End!' from Wordsworth, for instance."[15] Through his title Roethke refers us to the following passage from *The Prelude*:

> . . . there is a dark
> Inscrutable workmanship that reconciles
> Discordant elements, makes them cling together
> In one society. How strange that all
> The terrors, pains, and early miseries,
> Regrets, vexations, lassitudes, interfused
> Within my mind, should e'er have borne a part,
> And that a needful part, in making up
> The calm existence that is mine when I
> Am worthy of myself! Praise to the end!
>
> (Book I, 341-350)

Malkoff, in his only reference to Wordsworth in his book on Roethke's poetry, quotes part of the above passage and states that "this is precisely the point of view from which Roethke will consider his own childhood: an exploration of

[15] *Selected Letters*, pp. 229-230.

the ways in which spiritual ends are achieved through psychological means, how final peace is arrived at as a result of 'early miseries.' "[16] Roethke arrives at no "final peace"; in fact, the only thing "final" in all of *Praise to the End!* is "what footie does." The protagonist in Roethke's sequence "begin[s] from the depths and come[s] out,"[17] and that he does come out, that he survives, is the end which Roethke praises. The sentence beginning "How strange . . ." is not a declarative statement of the natural progression from means to an end, from "early miseries" to peace, but an exclamation expressing Wordsworth's amazement that all the turmoil of his experiences has resulted in an end deserving of praise—that the chaos of private experience has almost miraculously resulted in the order of a poem. The lines express wonder over the very process of moving from life into art. Roethke indeed will examine his childhood from the same perspective as Wordsworth: he will accept all kinds of experience and will with "dark/Inscrutable workmanship" make, at least in the aesthetic construct, a reconciliation between them. For both poets, the "early miseries" were not the cause of the present peace, but the materials out of which the poet shaped the present "calm existence."

The poet can use the idea of a tradition both to provide himself with models for his composition and to offer the reader a guide into his poetry. The many affinities between Roethke's autobiographical volume of fourteen poems and Wordsworth's *Prelude* in fourteen books show that Roethke was consciously selecting the *Prelude* to fulfill both functions. A minor but interesting similarity is that both poets wished to have their long sequences accepted as part of a tradition of oral poetry. "One of the most important differences between Wordsworth and the other major poets of the eighteenth and nineteenth centuries," F. W. Bateson writes, "is that whereas they wrote for the silent reader, *i.e.* for the eye, he wrote most of his poems to be declaimed, *i.e.*

[16] Karl Malkoff, p. 66.

[17] "Open Letter," p. 40.

for the ear."[18] Roethke instructs the reader of his poems to "*listen* to them, for they are written to be heard."[19]

In his Preface to *The Excursion*, Wordsworth described *The Prelude* as "the history of the Author's mind,"[20] beginning with childhood and schooltime and continuing to his residence in France during the Revolution. Roethke describes *Praise to the End!* as "the spiritual history of a protagonist"[21] and, in a telling but usually unnoticed letter, as ". . . a sequence of dramatic pieces beginning with a small child and working up. A kind of tensed-up *Prelude*, maybe: no comment; everything in the mind of the kid."[22] Wordsworth wished "almost [to] make remotest infancy/A visible scene" (I, 634-635), Roethke to "create a reality, a verisimilitude, the 'as if' of the child's world."[23] "Fair seed-time had my soul," Wordsworth wrote, "and I grew up/Fostered alike by beauty and by fear" (I, 301-302); and Roethke writes that his father's greenhouses, "a wonderful place for a child to grow up," were to him "both heaven and hell."[24] Both poets show the development of a child's mind and wish to bring into their poems not only the delights but also the terrors of childhood.

Some of the parallels noted above are between the actual circumstances of Roethke's and Wordsworth's lives; others are between the form and diction of Roethke's and Wordsworth's poetry. The two kinds of parallels show both the similarities between the poets and the processes by which Roethke related himself to Wordsworth. Roethke discovered the first type of correspondence through the act of reading prior to writing; he created the second type through the

[18] F. W. Bateson, *Wordsworth: A Re-interpretation* (London: Longmans, 1956), p. 187.

[19] "Open Letter," p. 37.

[20] *The Poetical Works of William Wordsworth*, v, 2.

[21] "An American Poet Introduces Himself," *On the Poet and His Craft*, p. 10.

[22] *Selected Letters*, p. 148.

[23] "An American Poet Introduces Himself," p. 10.

[24] "An American Poet . . . ," p. 8.

very act of writing. By composing poems similar to Wordsworth's, Roethke multiplies the number and kind of the parallels between himself and the earlier poet. The discovery of a tradition becomes the means to the creation of a tradition.

The organization of *The Prelude* and *Praise to the End!* is similar: both poets repeatedly liken the structure of their poems to a difficult journey.[25] Wordsworth travels over ". . . paths that, in the main,/Were more circuitous, but not less sure/Duly to reach the point marked out by Heaven" (VI, 751-753). "I believe," Roethke writes, "that the spiritual man must go back in order to go forward. The way is circuitous, and sometimes lost, but invariably returned to."[26] By using the journey as a structural metaphor, both poets attempt to move beyond the purely personal to trans-personal or even universal forms of experience. As in so many other Romantic poems, Wordsworth in *The Prelude* persistently attempts to universalize his own private experience, while Roethke refers to his series of long poems in these same terms: he wants "to catch the movement of the mind itself, to trace the spiritual history of a protagonist (not 'I' personally but of all haunted and harried men); to make this sequence a true and not arbitrary order. . . ."[27] In describing Section IV of "The Lost Son" ("a return to a memory of childhood"), Roethke writes that "the experience, again, is at once literal and symbolical."[28] The same reciprocal action between levels of meaning often occurs in Romantic poetry: there is a continual interplay between literal and metaphorical levels of meaning in *The Prelude*, particularly when Wordsworth describes a scene from his youth. Both poets take a childhood experience in the physical world and present it in their poems as not only a literal

[25] For Wordsworth, see Appendix Three in Herbert Lindenberger, *On Wordsworth's Prelude*. For Roethke, see "Open Letter," p. 39.

[26] "An American Poet . . . ," p. 12.

[27] "An American Poet . . . ," p. 10.

[28] "Open Letter," p. 38.

event in their adult memory but simultaneously a symbolic event transformed by the imagination, thereby moving beyond the limited significance of merely private experience to universal consequence.

In *The Prelude* and *Praise to the End!* there are sections of spiritual and visionary illumination—"spots of time" with "wonder heightened," as described by Wordsworth (XII, 208; VII, 153), moments of "heightened consciousness," as described by Roethke.[29] Wind and water, the controlling images of the two works, act as intermediaries between the visible world and this other world of higher vision. In the boat-stealing episode in Book I of *The Prelude*, the elements of the landscape—the moonlight, the water, and the mountains—remain a particularized setting experienced by the speaker, but as Wordsworth and the reader move beyond the outward circumstances into "huge and mighty Forms," we approach a visionary experience transcending the particular:

> Nor without the voice
> Of mountain-echoes did my boat move on;
> Leaving behind her still, on either side,
> Small circles glittering idly in the moon,
> Until they melted all into one track
> Of sparkling light. . . .
> I dipped my oars into the silent lake, . . .
> With trembling oars I turned,
> And through the silent water stole my way.
> (Book I, 362-367, 374, 385-386)

The situation in the following passage from Roethke's "The Shape of the Fire" is almost identical to that in Wordsworth's poem—a silent lake on which a solitary child rows a boat in the evening. Again, the water is part of the visible world, but by contemplating the water drops sliding from the oar and the water on which the boat drifts, Roethke and

[29] "On 'Identity,'" *On the Poet and His Craft*, p. 25.

the reader are led to an intense awareness of beauty and into the world of mystical experience:

> To stare into the after-light, the glitter
> left on the lake's surface,
> When the sun has fallen behind a wooded
> island;
> To follow the drops sliding down from the
> lifted oar,
> Held up, while the rower breathes, and
> the small boat drifts quietly shoreward;
> To know that light falls and fills, often
> without our knowing,
> As an opaque vase fills to the brim from
> a quick pouring,
> Fills and trembles at the edge yet does
> not flow over,
> Still holding and feeding the stem of the
> contained flower.
>
> (CP 67)

Not only are the settings and the mood of quiet tenseness the same in these two passages, but much of the vocabulary is also similar. What we and Roethke are finally observing here is not just the natural world, but also Wordsworth's poem. In fully appreciating Roethke's achievement, we must become aware of both the interaction between the poet's mind and those objects described in the poem and the interaction between Roethke and Wordsworth.

This same passage has many other Wordsworthian elements in it. I discussed earlier the lines from Book I of *The Prelude* in which Wordsworth writes that he "held unconscious intercourse with beauty/Old as creation, drinking in a pure/Organic pleasure. . . ." An image of drinking, in which quite literally outer becomes inner, is taken as a metaphor for the spiritual interchange between the poet and his world. Roethke's phrase "holding and feeding" presents a similar image of nourishment. The child is filled "to the brim" with pleasure ("drinking in a pure/Organic pleasure"), "without . . . knowing" it ("unconscious intercourse"). In addition, Roethke uses the same images of a boat and an island in his passage as Wordsworth does in many parts of *The Prelude* (for example, II, 54-65; II, 164-174). The way in which Wordsworth and Roethke conceive of boats and islands is an outcome of more than their own private perceptions; they are both making use of traditional *topoi*. As Herbert Lindenberger comments on this particular figure in *On Wordsworth's Prelude*: "the island (with its companion trope, the lone boat) is one of the great Romantic images, and to record its history from Saint-Pierre to Innisfree is to encompass much of the essential history of Romanticism."[30]

The many parallels in thought and technique between Roethke and Wordsworth, in addition to just the boat and island images, show that they are clearly working within the same tradition of Romantic poetry. Wordsworth universalizes personal experiences by embodying them in traditional literary motifs, and Roethke adds a trans-personal dimension to his private world through his development of and implicit references to a tradition in which Wordsworth is a central figure. Roethke's responsiveness to Wordsworth's poetry guides his own development while at the same time leading him to develop a new form of the tradition in which he and Wordsworth share.

My concern here has been with the milieu of poetry rather than with Roethke's intellectual milieu. Roethke of course picked up basic attitudes towards nature from other writers in the Wordsworthian tradition, including Emerson and Thoreau.[31] But, regardless of where or when in his read-

[30] Lindenberger, p. 80.

[31] Roethke's possible indebtedness to Emerson and Thoreau is explored in Hyatt H. Waggoner's *American Poets from the Puritans to the Present* (New York: Dell, 1968), pp. 564-577.

ing Roethke first met these ideas, it seems as though Wordsworth finally took the most important position in this tradition (just as he historically holds the pre-eminent position) since Roethke could respond with sympathetic imitation to Wordsworth's themes and techniques.

III

A Widening Sensibility

The titles of all six poems in Part I of *Praise to the End!* derive from the expanding sense of a literary heritage that Roethke was beginning to make his own.[1] Some have mistaken this eclecticism for an "eccentricity" detached from any tradition,[2] but this is clearly not the case. Christopher Smart's *chef-d'oeuvre*, "A Song to David," is the source for both the title and the basic structure of the first poem, "Where Knock Is Open Wide." Because Smart brought to his poem "a mind richly stored with information gathered from a variety of sources, some of which are not at all widely known,"[3] "A Song to David" appears complicated and obscure. As Robert Brittain explains, however, the actual difficulty and complexity of the poem lie not in its oblique allusiveness but "in Smart's technique of expression . . . in the sheer intellectual and artistic ingenuity with which the main themes are stated, elaborated, varied, and intensified by the manipulation of a number of minor themes around them."[4] Federico Olivero in "Il 'Canto a Davide' di Christopher Smart" points out that, in spite of these multiple variations, "each image is not independent of the others, but they respond from stanza to stanza in a harmony that

[1] Roethke has himself identified the source for three titles, but the remaining sources have not been previously noticed.

[2] See, for example, Joseph Bennett's review of *Praise to the End!* in *Hudson Review*, No. 7 (Summer, 1954), p. 305. "Eccentricity," he writes, is "the center from which the poems spring."

[3] *Poems by Christopher Smart*, ed. Robert Brittain (Princeton: Princeton University Press, 1950), Brittain's notes, pp. 292-293. Quotations from "A Song to David" are from this edition.

[4] Brittain's notes, p. 294.

echoes long and far."[5] Roethke's poem is also a "strange medley" with details and images gathered from various sources, including Smart's song. Just as Smart's poem contains "a prodigious multitude of animals, birds, fishes, reptiles, plants, and even stones,"[6] so Roethke's poem is filled with kittens, cows, puppies, ghoulies, mice, angels, ghosts, waterbirds, owls, bullheads, snakes, worms, frogs, roses, trees, and stones. His poem, like Smart's, seems at first disconnected, even chaotic, but actually it is constructed upon principles very similar to those in "A Song to David." Both poets employ the methods of musical arrangement—for example, elaboration of a motif and repetition of the same theme in various chords (i.e., expressing the same idea through many different images). Modern interpreters of Smart's poem, like Olivero, find it useful to employ musical terms to describe Smart. Similarly, Roethke describes the themes of his own long poems as "often coming alternately, as in music" with "usually a partial resolution at the end."[7]

The specific passage in which Roethke found his title ends

> And in the seat to faith assign'd,
> Where ask is have, where seek is find,
> Where knock is open wide.
> ("A Song to David," stanza LXXVII)

Ralph J. Mills, Jr. writes that "Roethke's piece, which presents the sensations and thoughts of earliest childhood, seems to use the line from Smart to imply birth and entry into the world. From this aspect Roethke's poem somewhat resembles Dylan Thomas' 'Before I Knocked.' "[8] Malkoff states that the line from Smart "refers to the literal, as well

[5] Federico Olivero, "Il 'Canto a Davide' di Christopher Smart," *Studi Brittanici* (Torino, 1931), pp. 105-126. Translated by Brittain and quoted in his notes to *Poems by Christopher Smart*, p. 296.

[6] Brittain's notes, p. 293.

[7] "Open Letter," p. 37.

[8] Ralph J. Mills, Jr., *Theodore Roethke* (Minneapolis: University of Minnesota Press, 1963), p. 18.

as the psychological or spiritual, birth of the child," and he too refers the reader to Thomas' poem.[9] But we cannot disregard Roethke's title, which clearly asks us to place his poem in the tradition of Smart, before attempting to find echoes in other poets. Smart and Roethke use "where knock is open wide" to image a psychic state where the normal kinds of causal relationships are collapsed and where the usual disjunction between desire and gratification does not occur. To Smart, this state of a complete identification between desire and fulfillment exists for the man of prayer; to Roethke, it exists for the child. For us, of course, Freud's studies support the idea that the psyche of the infant before he is born and even shortly afterwards is actually in this condition of identification. Because the very young child is immediately gratified in his desires, he does not experience the difference between cause and effect or between the self and the other; at first, for example, the child thinks that the mother's breast is part of himself.[10] The tension for the child (and the tension in Roethke's poem) begins when the identification begins to break down, when the child realizes that the world is not always responsive to his wishes, a process

[9] Malkoff, p. 70.

[10] Carolyn Kizer, in "Poetry of the Fifties in America" in *International Literary Annual*, ed. John Wain (London, 1958), p. 84, writes, "I should probably say here that Roethke has not read Joyce or Jung; and that, in 1952, after all his long poems exploring a child's history of consciousness had appeared, he was discovered in a Morris chair by a friend, with a copy of Freud's *Basic Writings* on one arm, his book *Praise to the End!* on the other, and his notebook in his lap, checking references, and chortling to himself, 'I was right! I was right!'" Roy Harvey Pearce ("Theodore Roethke: The Power of Sympathy," *Theodore Roethke: Essays on the Poetry*, ed. Stein, p. 179) answers that "One can only suppose that the friend mistook Winterset Rothberg [a pseudonym Roethke occasionally used for satirical prose pieces] for Theodore Roethke. . . . I must state flatly that the poems are supersaturated with language out of Freud and Jung, or their myriad exegetes." Like Pearce, I am making no attempt to claim any particular work by Freud as a source for Roethke's poems, but rather I am placing Roethke's works in the modern poet's milieu, of which various Freudian and pseudo-Freudian ideas are a part.

that begins almost immediately after birth. In late childhood and up until adolescence, there may still be vestiges of identification of self and other in the child's perception and appreciation of nature.

Two pre-Freudian poets who seem to have been working with some of these same concepts are Blake and Wordsworth. For Blake, in the state of innocence there is no conflict between self and other and no repression. The fall into division occurs when the child grows up into the state of experience in which man's spiritual nature is at odds with his material surroundings. Wordsworth believes that "the infant Babe" is "no outcast . . . , bewildered and depressed," since

> Along his infant veins are interfused
> The gravitation and the filial bond
> Of nature that connect him with the world.
> (*Prelude*, Book II, 242-244)

Wordsworth finds that as the child moves from infancy to early adolescence, he maintains evidences of this primal unity in his lively imagination, which sees correspondences between the inner life of the self and the outer life of nature. Wordsworth, Blake, and Freud are all part of the background to which Roethke implicitly refers in his poem.

"Where Knock Is Open Wide" is written from the perspective of a small child. Just as he does not recognize the adult division of cause and effect, the child does not acknowledge the normal patterns of language that tend to divide our vision of the world. The poem begins, "A kitten can/Bite with his feet." There are certain words in English we can use to describe what a kitten can do with his feet, and others we cannot use; thus we have already divided the world of words into two groups. In that category of words we cannot use to describe what a kitten can do with his feet is the word "bite." If a poet wants to define through the method of his poetry that state of childhood innocence in which divisions do not exist, then in the language of his poem he must select a word from the "can't use" group and use it. Of course many words that the poet could choose would not make any sense at all; Roethke therefore picks a word (bite) that is associated with the proper word (scratch, for instance) in order to communicate an idea of a cat's actions and at the same time to show in the very structure of the language of his poem a breakdown of categories to suggest that childhood is the state of the human soul in which man overcomes divisions and attains a unity. By using "bite" with "feet," Roethke not only gives an image of the state of innocence, but also reveals something about the very nature of poetry: all poetry is a process of breaking down the normal divisions of straightforward, logical discourse to reach a new unity between things, qualities, or actions that are normally thought to be different. Roethke, through his verbal structures, makes statements about both the human condition of innocence and the condition of poetry. Perhaps the final unity that he achieves is writing about the nature of man and the nature of poetry simultaneously.

The title and the first sentence of "Where Knock Is Open Wide" establish the basic patterns repeated in the poem, whereby the usual categories of language and logic are not observed. In the line, "I know it's an owl. He's making it darker," the child transposes cause and effect: darkness, of course, causes the owl to come out, but for the child the owl causes the darkness to come. When the child says, "Hello happy hands," he transfers the emotions of the perceiver into the perceived, as if no such division existed. The expressions "I'll be a bite. You be a wink" show that the child sees a union between the person who performs the action and the action itself. He has a total sympathy with everything because he is one with all things: "I was sad for a fish." Since for the child there is no division among the five faculties, he makes sense-transferences: like Blake's man in the state of innocence who says, "I heard a wild flower," Roethke's child says, "I hear flowers." The consciousness of the child also makes no distinctions between real events and dreams: "Maybe I'm lost,/ Or asleep." These basic patterns central to the construction of the poem are first brought to the reader's attention through the title. Although a good portion of his poem is based upon a violation of the conventional patterns of logic and discourse, Roethke, by consciously choosing Smart's line as the title for his poem, directs the reader to see even his break with tradition as itself part of a tradition. Smart's line is the whole poem in microcosm.

Almost as soon as the infant is born, of course, the learning process begins. The child starts to divide the world into various categories—the self and the other, here and there, cause and effect—and to learn that in this world all desires are not fulfilled. Similarly, the breakdown of unity begins very early in Roethke's poem. Since the state of innocence is shown through images of unity, the fall into experience is shown through images of disunion: "Ask" is no longer "have," as in Smart; instead, the child asks, "How high is have?" "Seek" is no longer "find"; "God's somewhere else,/ I said to Mamma."

While these images of the fall into division do begin to occur in "Where Knock Is Open Wide," they play a much larger role in the second poem of the sequence, "I Need, I Need," which presents a further stage of infancy. Roethke's title is similar to Blake's inscription "I Want! I Want!" for the ninth design in his series *For Children: The Gates of Paradise* (1793), which, like Wordsworth's *Prelude* and Roethke's *Praise to the End!*, traces the history of man as he develops from an infant to an adult. Both Blake and Roethke are writing about that same condition of childhood where there is an awakening of desire for all sorts of things that are out of the child's reach or, at the very least, that are no longer seen as part of the self. Roethke begins his poem with the child's extremely basic desire for food:

A deep dish. Lumps in it.
I can't taste my mother.
Hoo. I know the spoon.
Sit in my mouth.

(CP 74)

The mother's breast has been taken away from the child: The immediate and perfect response to his desire for food is no longer present. The child has reached the state where knock is not open wide: there is now a division of desires into two types—those fulfilled and those not fulfilled.

The Trouble is with No and Yes
As you can see I guess I guess.

The words "yes" and "no" are the linguistic equivalents, and results, of this categorization of desires.

Blake's design for "I Want! I Want!" shows a child reaching for the moon, an action signifying a desire for something impossible to acquire. The child of "I Need, I Need" has longings equally impossible to fulfill:

I wish I was a pifflebob
I wish I was a funny
I wish I had ten thousand hats,
And made a lot of money.

Blake and Roethke are working with concepts of innocence and experience, and both define these two states in terms of the child's relationship between the self and the other, with desire as the operative emotion that attempts to link the two. In *Songs of Innocence and of Experience*, Blake makes his primary distinction between the two states on the basis of the relationship between the child and his natural surroundings, which in innocence is one of harmony: the child plays with the lamb ("The Lamb,"

"Spring"), the meadows laugh in response to the laughter of the children ("Laughing Song," "Nurse's Song"), and the child sleeps with "tygers wild" ("The Little Girl Found"). In experience there is an alienation between the child and nature, between the self and the other: "The Ecchoing Green" becomes "the darkening Green"; the night is dark, the mire deep, and the child becomes a lost son. The child longs for objects and pleasures that he cannot grasp because nature is no longer in harmony with the self. Since the moon is an image of these things far out of the reach of the child, Blake's design in *The Gates of Paradise* is a perfect emblem for the disjunction between self and other: it is the Blakean version of the vanity of human wishes. The wishes of the child in "I Need, I Need" are equally vain. In the previous poem he could say, "I'll be a bite. You be a wink," but now he can only wish he could be "a pifflebob" and "a funny."

Roethke has characterized the tone of Part 2, which begins with two children jumping rope, as one of "mingled longing and aggressiveness."[11] The longing occurs because the self desires the other; the aggression develops because the other is not part of the self and cannot be controlled by the self. The division finally leads to hostility, which only increases the alienation between the two children:

> Not you I need.
> Go play with your nose.
> Stay in the sun,
> Snake-eyes.

Both poets make use of the same movement from union to disunion, from harmony to disharmony, to describe and symbolize the growth of the child. By consciously relating himself to Blake, Roethke places himself within a tradition of poetry notable for its conceptual complexity in spite of the simplicity of its diction. Modern Blake criticism has

11 "An American Poet Introduces Himself," *On the Poet and His Craft*, p. 10.

been particularly successful in elucidating his lyrics by paying close attention not so much to the meanings of individual words as to the conceptual basis for the arrangement of the words. Roethke's "I Need, I Need" must be read in the same way. Even finding the exact meaning of the word "pifflebob" would not tell us very much about Roethke's poem. We can only discover Roethke's meaning, his images of innocence and experience, through an understanding of the reasons for the patterns resulting from his peculiar linguistic junctions and disjunctions.

In addition to being the main character and the leading symbol in these particular works, the child is also Blake's and Roethke's proposed audience. They implicitly refer to the Gospel pronouncement asking that men "become as little children" to enter into the kingdom of heaven (Matthew 18:3). Blake wrote in a letter to the Reverend Dr. Trusler, "You say that I want somebody to Elucidate my Ideas. . . . But I am happy to find a Great Majority of Fellow Mortals who can Elucidate My Visions, & Particularly they have been Elucidated by Children, who have taken a greater delight in contemplating my Pictures than I even hoped."[12] Roethke wrote in his "Open Letter," ". . . believe me: you will have no trouble if you approach these poems as a child would, naïvely, with your whole being awake, your faculties loose and alert."[13]

Blake and Roethke belong to a very small group of poets who have successfully spoken from the perspective of the child and in his language. Both shunned what Roethke in "Open Letter" contemptuously termed "cutesy prattle" and "a suite in goo-goo." Their poems exemplify a line from Blake's *Milton* (plate 30), a line Roethke wrote down in one of his notebooks in 1946: "How wide the Gulf & Unpassable! between Simplicity & Insipidity."[14] The two poets

[12] *Blake Complete Writings*, ed. Geoffrey Keynes (London: Oxford University Press, 1966), pp. 793-794. All further quotations from Blake's works are from this edition.

[13] "Open Letter," p. 37.

[14] Theodore Roethke Collection, University of Washington, Seattle (Notebooks, Box 37, #97).

also avoid that often condescending perspective from which an adult describes a child. As S. Foster Damon has demonstrated, Blake "does not contemplate children, in the manner of Wordsworth, Hugo, and Longfellow; he actually enters into their souls and speaks through their own mouths."[15] Similarly, Roethke's poems are written "entirely from the viewpoint of a very small child: all interior drama; no comment; no interpretation."[16]

Since Blake's songs and Roethke's poems are in the child's voice, the words are those a child would use—mainly monosyllabic, familiar, concrete, native, and active. When the state of innocence is evoked by a speaker who is himself not in innocence, the language is quite different. In Blake's "Holy Thursday," the speaker is aware of the disparity between the innocence of the children and the world of experience in which they live, and accordingly the language is not the simple Anglo-Saxon diction of a child, but the polysyllabic, Latinate vocabulary of an adult. Roethke makes this same sort of shift in diction, and thus simultaneously makes a transfer from the perspective of the infant to that of the adult, when he begins to use phrases such as "pelludious Jesus-shimmer" and "dangerous indignation" in "O, Thou Opening, O." The viewpoint and the final significance of many of Blake's and Roethke's poems about childhood become very complex because the two contrary states of innocence and experience are not mutually exclusive and can exist in the same child or the same poem at once.

The only counterparts to the strongly stressed rhythms of Blake and Roethke are found in those very poems most closely associated with childhood—nursery rhymes. "Mother Goose's songs," as they were titled in the eighteenth century,[17] could quite naturally provide Blake with the raw materials for his own evocations of innocence since the

[15] S. Foster Damon, *William Blake: His Philosophy and Symbols* (London: Constable and Company, 1924), pp. 40-41.

[16] "Open Letter," p. 41.

[17] *The Oxford Dictionary of Nursery Rhymes*, ed. Iona and Peter Opie (Oxford: Clarendon Press, 1951), p. 1. All following quotations of nursery rhymes are taken from this edition unless otherwise noted.

songs, if not actually the products of children, are the expressions of that part of the soul which Blake identifies with innocence. Damon asks, "was Blake's own ear responsible for his original and instinctive cadences (which were quite unlike anything in the poetry of his day), or was he imitating the queer, yet satisfactory, metres of *Mother Goose*?" Damon answers his own question when he writes that "already in *An Island in the Moon* Blake had quoted *The Froggy would awooing ride*; and in the *Jerusalem* (of all places!) we find an unmistakable reminiscence of *Fa, fe, fi, fo, fum*!

> Boys and girls, come out to play,
> The moon does shine as bright as day

is strangely parallel in spirit to the *Nurse's Song*. Certainly, nothing in Blake's day approaches his *Songs* metrically, except *Mother Goose*."[18] Although Damon primarily points out parallels between the meters of nursery songs and Blake's songs, there are also close resemblances in the rhymes. Compare, for example, Blake's "The Blossom" in which the flower sees the sparrow "swift as arrow" with the following lines of "Who Killed Cock Robin?":

> I said the Sparrow,
> With my bow and arrow . . .

The endings of the two songs are also quite similar:

> A happy Blossom
> Hears you sobbing, sobbing
> Pretty, Pretty Robin.
> (Blake, "The Blossom")

> All the birds of the air
> Fell a-sighing and a-sobbing,
> When they heard the bell toll
> For poor Cock Robin.
> ("Who Killed Cock Robin?")

[18] Damon, p. 42.

Having seen what Blake was able to do with nursery rhymes in *Songs of Innocence*, Roethke turned not only to Blake in "I Need, I Need," but also to the tradition of nursery rhymes common to both poets. "Rhythmically," Roethke wrote, "it's the spring and rush of the child I'm after."[19] He found this energetic rhythm in the strongly stressed, irregular metrical patterns of Mother Goose and employed it in the jump-rope section of "I Need, I Need":

Even steven all is less:
I haven't time for sugar,
Put your finger in your face,
And there will be a booger.

A one is a two is
I know what you is:
You're not very nice,—
So touch my toes twice.

I know you are my nemesis
So bibble where the pebble is.
The Trouble is with No and Yes
As you can see I guess I guess.

I wish I was a pifflebob
I wish I was a funny
I wish I had a thousand hats,
And made a lot of money.

Open a hole and see the sky:
A duck knows something
You and I don't.
Tomorrow is Friday.

In addition to using the "sprung" rhythm of the nursery jingle, Roethke borrows other devices: the short line, internal rhymes within the verses ("bibble," "pebble," "trouble"), the command ("Go play with your nose"), and "repetition in word and phrase and in idea," which, according

[19] "Open Letter," p. 41.

to Roethke, "is the very essence of poetry and particularly of *this* kind of poetry."[20] Roethke uses these devices common to nursery rhymes not only to suggest childhood, but also to evoke directly the mood of the nursery rhymes themselves: nursery rhyming is both a basic technique employed in this poem and a part of the very subject matter and themes with which this poem deals.

In addition to this general use of nursery rhyme techniques, Roethke borrows words and images from specific rhymes, particularly those which are the oldest and the most widely known. Roethke's taunt "Put your finger in your face,/And there will be a booger" calls to mind the old gibe "Cry, baby cry,/Put your finger in your eye,/ And tell your mother it wasn't I," which Iona and Peter Opie in *The Lore and Language of Schoolchildren* cite as the jeer "most often repeated both in Britain and the United States" and as one of the many verses to "have been helping tears to flow faster for generations."[21] "Dance, Thumbkin, Dance," a well-known infants' game played with the fingers, is the source for the line "Bumpkin, he can dance alone" in Part I of "Praise to the End!" "Dish," "spoon," and "diddle" in the first two stanzas of "I Need, I Need" echo the words of the poem that the editors of *The Oxford Dictionary of Nursery Rhymes* refer to as "probably the best-known nonsense verse in the language," "Hey Diddle Diddle."[22] When Roethke in "The Lost Son" implores, "Snail, snail, glister me forward," he directs the reader to

[20] "Some Remarks on Rhythm," *On the Poet and His Craft*, p. 77. On p. 79 of this essay Roethke writes about the rhythm that is produced by playing against an established meter and he uses Blake's "A Poison Tree" as an example: "The whole poem is a masterly example of variation in rhythm. . . . It's what Blake called 'the bounding line,' the nervousness, the tension, the energy in the whole poem." When Blake used the phrase "the bounding line," he was actually writing about the boundary line between objects in drawings and engravings, and not about a technique in rhythm. But, as usual, Roethke is interpreting or even misinterpreting for his own uses.

[21] Iona and Peter Opie, *The Lore and Language of Schoolchildren* (Oxford: Clarendon Press, 1959), p. 188.

[22] *The Oxford Dictionary of Nursery Rhymes*, p. 203.

the nursery rhyme "Snail, snail, come out of your hole . . . Snail, snail, put out your horns . . . ," a chant that, according to the Opies, is "comparable with 'Ladybird, Ladybird, fly away home' in its inexplicableness and probable antiquity. . . . Whatever is the significance of the snail to engender such invocations, it must lie deep in the history of the world. The diversity of languages in which the rhyme is found is almost unparalleled."[23]

Roethke has written that there are some words such as "hill," "plow," "mother," "window," "bird," "fish" that are "drenched with human association"[24]—an accurate statement as applied to single words, but one hazardous to apply to any particular poems, with the possible exception of these familiar nursery rhymes, said and sung often without alteration for many generations. By using these primal and universally evocative poems, Roethke creates the kind of poetry he describes as "shot through with appeals to the unconsciousness, to the fears and desires that go far back into our childhood, into the imagination of the race."[25] Also, snatches and phrases from lullabies, counting-out rhymes, singing games, nonsense jingles, retorts, charms, and skip-rope poems that have been transmitted by word of mouth from generation to generation introduce an oral dimension into Roethke's printed poem, suggesting basic speech and song patterns to the reader. Just as Roethke refers back to childhood, the reader must make a similar journey back into his own childhood experiences in order to recall those nursery rhymes to which the poet alludes. The reader must actively participate in the final shaping of the poem's meaning: he not only must use the specific lines given in Roethke's poem, but also must rely upon his own knowledge of the tradition of poetry from which Roethke's lines spring.

Blake and Roethke were further attracted and inspired

[23] *The Oxford Dictionary of Nursery Rhmyes*, pp. 390-391.
[24] "Some Remarks on Rhythm," p. 80.
[25] *Ibid.*

by the absolute and unmatched nastiness of a large portion of Mother Goose. Nursery rhymes, like Blake's songs, show the two contrary states of the human soul: many a soothing lullaby has as its counterpart a poem of disturbing maliciousness. The similar titles and rhymes of "Rock-a-bye, Baby" and "Jumbo had a Baby" only serve to emphasize the disparity between the innocence of one and the cunning of the other:

Rock-a-bye, baby,
Thy cradle is green,
Father's a nobleman,
Mother's a queen.
(Opie, p. 62)

Jumbo had a baby
All dressed in green.
Jumbo didn't like it
Sent it to the Queen.

The Queen did not like it
Because it was so fat,
Cut it up in slices
And gave it to the cat.
(Opie, pp. 200-201)

The tone of gleeful viciousness inherent in poems like "Jumbo had a Baby" caused nursery rhyme reformers (beginning with George Wither in 1641 and continuing to the present day) to protest that many rhymes are not suitable for children's ears. The editors of *The Annotated Mother Goose* discuss one of the more ardent leaders of the Reformation: "In 1925 Mrs. Winifred Sackville Stoner, Jr., once a child prodigy who used a typewriter at the age of three, tried to attack Mother Goose constructively by promulgating informative jingles, rhymes that 'represent life.' Example: Every perfect person owns/Just two hundred and six bones."[26] As poems about bones go, this one hardly compares either in rhythm or memorability to the nursery rhyme about the single mutton bone belonging to a far from "perfect person":

[26] William S. Baring-Gould and Ceil Baring-Gould, *The Annotated Mother Goose* (New York: Clarkson N. Potter, 1962), p. 19.

Hannah Bantry, in the pantry,
Gnawing at a mutton bone;
How she gnawed it,
How she clawed it,
When she found herself alone.
(Opie, p. 198)

In 1952 another reformer, Geoffrey Handley-Taylor, wrote that at least half of traditional nursery rhymes "harbour unsavoury elements," and he made a long list of the incidents that occur in the average Mother Goose collection, such as "allusion to murder," "killing domestic animals," "devouring human flesh," and "physical violence."[27] Rather than trying to remove "the unsavoury elements" from nursery rhymes, Blake and Roethke are perhaps the only two poets who relished them and have tried to preserve them in their contributions to the tradition of nursery rhymes:

And this he always kept in mind,
And form'd a crooked knife,
And ran about with bloody hands
To seek his mother's life. . . .

He took up fever by the neck
And cut out all its spots,
And thro' the holes which he had made
He first discover'd guts.
(from *An Island in the Moon*, chapter 6)

Is it soft like a mouse?
Can it wrinkle its nose?
Could it come in the house
On the tips of its toes?

Take the skin of a cat
And the back of an eel,
Then roll them in grease,—
That's the way it would feel.
(from "The Lost Son," Part 1)

[27] *The Annotated Mother Goose*, p. 20.

Although nursery rhyme patterns continue to determine the rhythm in the first few stanzas of "Bring the Day!" the poem is primarily an investigation of some of Wordsworth's basic ideas, particularly as embodied in Book IV (Despondency Corrected) of *The Excursion*, from which Roethke derived his title:

> The unimprisoned Mind
> May yet have scope to range among her own,
> Her thoughts, her images, her high desires.
> If the dear faculty of sight should fail,
> Still, it may be allowed me to remember
> What visionary powers of eye and soul
> In youth were mine; when stationed on the top
> Of some huge hill—expectant, I beheld
> The sun rise up, from distant climes returned
> Darkness to chase, and sleep; and *bring the day* . . . [28]
> (IV, 106-115)

Both poets are dealing in their poems with three initially independent worlds—the world of the speaker, the world of nature, and the spiritual world—and are investigating the interactions among them. Wordsworth's Wanderer finds a complete harmony among these three existences, and he explains in considerable detail how he has corrected his despondency through the proper relationship to nature, which has led him finally to the proper relationship with God and with "the spiritual presences of absent things" (IV, 1234). Roethke looks at the harmony the Wanderer has attained and wonders if it is possible for him to arrive at this Wordsworthian concord. Through questioning the Wanderer's statements, he tries to find his own interrelationships among these three worlds. Roethke's attitude towards Wordsworth is ambiguous: he sees the value in the Wanderer's solution, and at the same time he questions its valid-

[28] *The Poetical Works of William Wordsworth*, ed. E. de Selincourt (Oxford: Clarendon Press, 1949), V, 112-113. All subsequent quotations from *The Excursion* are from this edition.

ity. His own poem is filled with statements and counterstatements, with suggested methods for attaining a harmony, followed by rejections of those methods. The Wanderer finally leads us to definite statements about religious doctrine; Roethke is unwilling (or unable) to move from the vague spiritual feelings that he achieves through his relationship with nature to theological doctrine and institutionalized religion. He finds it impossible to define the specific quality of those spiritual presences in order to develop a theology, and instead he sets out to develop and accept his complex but assured relationship with nature.

Roethke begins his poem with an image of the harmony of nature:

Bees and lilies there were,
Bees and lilies there were,
Either to other,—
Which would you rather?
Bees and lilies were there.
(CP 77)

There is a complete interdependence between the bees and the lilies. It makes no difference which is called "either," which "other," since they rely equally on one another for existence, though less "through dependence upon mutual aid/Than by participation of delight," as Wordsworth writes of a similar situation (*Excursion*, IV, 442-443). The child wants to be part of this reciprocal relationship, to have an intimate union with the earth (the "she" of the poem):

The green grasses,—would they?
The green grasses?—
She asked her skin
To let me in:
The far leaves were for it.

The speaker has reached the stage of childhood in which there are distinctions between the self and the other. He is no longer in that infantile state where all the world seems part of himself; he is now beginning to realize that he is part of the world. The primal and egocentric unity of the infant is being replaced by this secondary form of unity, which is not egocentric and which forces the child outside of himself. This very process whereby the child moves outward to identify himself with the other is the radical experience that Wordsworth strives to define in much of his poetry. Poems such as *The Excursion*, in which Wordsworth moves outward from the isolation of the individual self to find solace through a bond with the greater life of nature, reenact that archetypal process.

Everything in Roethke's poem (including the structure)[29] is bound together, not through the self-centered perception of the infant, but, like the lily and the bee, in the cycles of nature. The child is starting to see that "Everything's closer." He asks, "Is this a cage?" The Wanderer referred to his "unimprisoned Mind," but the speaker here wonders if he is trapped in these interconnections among all things in nature and if this kind of confinement is desirable or not. Wordsworth would say that it was good: ". . . see/How Nature hems you in with friendly arms!/And by her help you are my prisoners still" (*Excursion*, Book III, 13-15). But Blake, whose ideas are now becoming important for Roethke, finds it a restriction of man's spirit that we are all locked in vegetal cycles and bound to death. Unlike the Wanderer, who is continually "answering the question which himself had asked" (IV, 68), Roethke does not answer his query ("Is this a cage?"), but he has started to inquire into his desire for a marriage between himself and nature: he is testing the turth of the Wordsworthian experience. Although the earth "asked her skin/To let me in," he now

[29] The poem moves from spring ("bees and lilies") to summer ("the green grasses"), to fall ("The chill's gone from the moon"—harvest moon; "The woods are alive" with color), to winter ("the white weather"), back to spring ("rain"), and ends with summer ("The spiders sail into summer").

says, "I can't marry the dirt." He also questions whether a feeling of communion with nature can lead to a spiritual communion. He senses spiritual presences, but can define them only in terms of what they are not:

And over by Algy's
Something came by me,
It wasn't a goose,
It wasn't a poodle.

Part 2 begins with another image of the harmonies within nature, an even more complex correlation than between the bees and the lilies:

The herrings are awake.
What's all the singing between?—
Is it with whispers and kissing?—
I've listened into the least waves.
The grass says what the wind says:
Begin with the rock;
End with water.

This passage, with its imagery of singing and whispering, rocks and water, is similar to the following lines from Book IV of the *Excursion*:

Nature fails not to provide
Impulse and utterance. The whispering air
Sends inspiration from the shadowy heights,
And blind recesses of the caverned rocks;
The little rills, and waters numberless,
Inaudible by daylight, blend their notes
With the loud streams.

(IV, 1169-1175)

While Wordsworth explicitly states that nature provides "impulse and utterance" and then proceeds to give examples, Roethke questions the significance of those natural harmonies in which Wordsworth finds delight in order to discover if the connections between the natural objects are based on love ("Is it with whispers and kissing?") rather than just on a cycle of cause and effect.

When Roethke writes, "The worm and the rose/Both love/Rain," he introduces a quite different union than that mutually productive one between the bee and the lily: but even though the immediate relationship is the destruction of the rose by the worm, when properly perceived they are somehow linked in a natural harmony. In spite of the destructive relationship that often exists between natural objects and between man and nature ("The white weather hates me"), at least there is a definable bond among all those things mentioned in Roethke's poem and among those objects and the speaker.

Finally, in the last stanza we get a movement from apathy and dejection to "despondency corrected." There is no logical progression between the questions asked in the first two parts of the poem and the announcement of a beginning at the end of the poem, but if we see Roethke's poem as a reworking of sections of Book IV of the *Excursion*, then we can understand the reason for Roethke's sudden leap from circuitous questionings to the forceful and assured tone at the end of his poem. The "beginning" at the end is a response not to the first sections of his own poem, but rather to Wordsworth's correction of despondency in *The Excursion*:

> O small bird wakening,
> Light as a hand among blossoms,
> Hardly any old angels are around any more.
> The air's quiet under the small leaves.
> The dust, the long dust, stays.
> The spiders sail into summer.
> It's time to begin!
> To begin!

After all the questionings, Roethke ends with certitude. "It's time to begin" his own excursion.

The title of the next poem in the series, "Give Way, Ye Gates," is the logical first step of the "beginning" announced at the end of the previous poem. In the initial line, "Believe me, knot of gristle, I bleed like a tree" (CP 79), the youth addressing his body is still at that early stage of adolescence in which his bones have not yet hardened. He identifies himself with growing vegetative life, as he did in "Bring the Day!" by stating, "When I stand, I'm almost a tree." Here he compares his blood with the sap of trees, suggesting that he is full of the energy and vitality of nature. The poem continues with a series of images that center on words emphasizing sensuous, physical existence. Studying these bodily images in isolation, we may have difficulty in finding the total pattern into which they are structured; but if we investigate the source of the title, as surely we are supposed to, we find a key to Roethke's intentions. "Give Way, Ye Gates" is from the first line of Robert Herrick's "The Wassaile,"[30] a poem celebrating and blessing the life of the senses. Herrick's wassailer and the reveler in Roethke's poem, both filled with youthful physical energies, want the gates to "give way" that they may enter into and praise the natural world of fertility and fruitfulness. The child in "Bring the Day!" was just awakening to nature; here, as an adolescent, he wants an involvement in nature. The image from the earlier poem of a "small bird wakening,/Light as a hand among blossoms" becomes "A bird sings in the bush of your bones." The tentative experiences are now realized. Besides all of these images from natural life, Roethke's vocabulary here suggests music, singing, and dancing, since he, like Herrick, sees the life of nature as a great festival.

A knowledge of Herrick's poem keeps the reader from misinterpreting many of the images. Malkoff, for instance, suggests that "Mother of blue" is a reference to the Virgin.[31]

[30] *The Poetical Works of Robert Herrick*, ed. L. C. Martin (Oxford: Clarendon Press, 1956), p. 178. All subsequent quotations from Herrick's poems are from this edition.

[31] Malkoff, p. 81.

In a poem extolling fecundity, however, the speaker calls not upon the Virgin, but upon Nature, mother of the blue sky and the blue sea. The speaker also addresses her as "Mother of . . . the many changes of hay," thereby referring to the cyclic movement of nature. The mood of Roethke's poem, like that of Herrick's, is pagan rather than Christian, celebrative rather than devotional. The child sees himself as married to Nature, as sharing in the festival of the senses: "We're king and queen of the right ground." Roethke finds in other poems by Herrick themes and images lauding the life of the senses and he brings them into this poem. He intensifies the *carpe diem* theme: we will not just seize the day, he says, "We'll swinge the instant!" Herrick's phrase "the happy dawning of her thigh"[32] becomes, in Roethke's poem, "In the high-noon of thighs," imaging the prospects of a full sexual life. Roethke characteristically out-Herricks Herrick.

In the final sections of "The Wassaile" and "Give Way, Ye Gates," Herrick and Roethke turn from a celebration of the senses to a realization of the inevitable dissolution of all physical life. Both poets image the body as a house. The gates to the senses that were opened are now closed, and, as Herrick writes, "Rust and cobwebs bind the gate." Everything is dried up and decayed: the flowing pans in the dairies of Herrick's poem have ceased to flow; there is neither "Ale or Beere"; "In a drie-house all things are neere." In the early parts of Roethke's poem we find "great milk," "slow rain," and "the water's loose," but, at the end, all has become waste and arid: "The dead crow dries on a pole." Both houses, like dead bodies, are now cold. "Chimneys do for ever weepe,/For want of warmth . . ." in Herrick's poem. For Roethke, what life finally comes to is "a cold scrape in a low place." ("Scrape" echoes the harsh, grating sound of the rusty gate in Herrick's poem and also echoes the sense of "neere," since "to scrape" and "to be neere" both mean "to hoard up penuriously.") Roethke's

[32] "The Vision," *The Poetical Works of Robert Herrick*, p. 51.

image of life reduced to its essential realities ("Touch and arouse. Suck and sob. Curse and mourn.") resembles Sweeney's remarks in Eliot's *Sweeney Agonistes*: "Birth, and copulation, and death./That's all the facts when you come to brass tacks." Herrick implies, and Roethke shows explicitly, that the final vision of life includes sterility, sadness, decay, and death. Thus, Roethke's poem ends, not as Malkoff suggests with "a kind of farewell to the time of union with nature,"[33] but with an acceptance of the whole course of nature and man, accepting both "what might be" and "what we are."

The final effect Herrick achieves at the conclusion of his poem is a view that recognizes the duality of all experience. He celebrates the life of the body, but he also recognizes that it can and finally must end. Roethke attempts to reach this same balanced view in his own poem, and the last two lines sum up his final attitude towards the life of the senses: "What slides away/Provides." Not only do all the things that provide sensuous pleasure slide away, but it is those very things which slide away that support the life of the senses and prepare against death.

After his consideration of the life of the senses and all that it implies in "Give Way, Ye Gates," in the next poem Roethke moves on to the theme of sensibility. Without knowing the source, and therefore the context, of the title "Sensibility! O La!" it is impossible to determine what Roethke means by the puzzling word "sensibility." That the word allows of more than one interpretation Roethke was well aware, for he often employed it in his prose writings with all of its ambiguities intact, to the extent even of using the word twice and with antonymous meanings in the same paragraph: "I think of my more tedious contemporaries: . . . those life-hating hacks, the critics without sensibility, masters of a castrated prose, readers of one book by any given author (or excerpts thereof), aware of one kind of effect, lazy dishonest arrogant generalisers, tasteless antholo-

[33] Malkoff, p. 82.

gists, their lists of merit, their values changing with every whim and wind of academic fashion; wimble-wamble essayists; philosophers without premise, bony blue-stocking commentators, full of bogus learning; horse-faced lady novelists, mere slop-jars of sensibility."[34]

The reason Roethke can revile a critic for not having any sensibility and simultaneously berate a novelist for having too much is that in each instance he is using the literary term differently. In the first phrase, he depends upon the modern definition of the word: "Today the term *sensibility* suggests highly developed emotional and intellectual apprehension and particularly a responsiveness to aesthetic phenomena . . . this word has been used by a number of the New Critics to describe qualities of the temperaments which produce or appreciate poetry."[35] By the phrase, "slop-jars of sensibility," Roethke refers to the over-wrought emotionalism in the literature of sensibility which M. H. Abrams describes as "a particular cultural phenomenon of the eighteenth century":

"The philosophical background of this tendency was the moral theory that developed as a reaction against seventeenth century Stoicism, which emphasized reason and the unemotional will as the motive to virtue, and even more importantly, as a reaction against Thomas Hobbes's theory that man is innately selfish, and that the springs of his behavior are self-interest and the drive to power. Sermons, essays, fiction, and philosophical writings . . . proclaimed that benevolence, or wishing others well, is innate in man; that virtue is mainly spontaneous action in response to this natural emotion; and that the most important ethical experience is that of sympathy and fellow feeling, or a hair-trigger responsiveness to the joys and distresses of other people. It became a commonplace in popular morality that

[34] "A Tirade Turning," *On the Poet and His Craft*, pp. 151-152. See also Roethke's references to sensibility on pages 88 ("hyenas of sensibility") and 100 ("A great roaring sensibility on the loose").

[35] Karl Beckson and Arthur Ganz, *A Reader's Guide to Literary Terms* (New York: Farrar, Straus and Cudahy, 1960), p. 189.

the ability to shed a sympathetic tear is the sign both of polite breeding and a virtuous heart."[36]

In order to understand the multiple uses of the term "sensibility" in Roethke's poems, it is necessary to trace the background of the specific work from which Roethke took his title. Many of the lines from Cowper's poem "Addressed to Miss —— on Reading and Prayer for Indifference" (1762) illustrate this literature of sensibility:

'Tis woven in the world's great plan,
And fix'd by heav'n's decree,
That all the true delights of man
Should spring from Sympathy. . . .

Oh! grant kind heav'n to me,
Long as I draw ethereal air,
Sweet sensibility.[37]

Laurence Sterne's *A Sentimental Journey* (1768) apostrophizes sensibility: "—Dear Sensibility! source inexhausted of all that's precious in our joys, or costly in our sorrows!" Sterne gives as an example of one who has sensibility a peasant whose "gentle heart . . . bleeds" over a "lacerated lamb": "Peace to thee, generous swain!—I see thou walkest off with anguish—but thy joys shall balance it—for happy is thy cottage— . . . and happy are the lambs which sport about you."[38]

The poem that ridicules these sentimental literary works collectively and that derides Sterne's passage particularly is a nineteenth-century nursery rhyme:

Dear Sensibility, O la!
I heard a little lamb cry, baa!
Says I, "So you have lost Mamma?"
"Ah!"

[36] M. H. Abrams, *A Glossary of Literary Terms* (New York: Holt, Rinehart, and Winston, 1957), p. 87.

[37] *Cowper: Poetical Works*, ed. H. S. Milford (London: Oxford University Press, 1934), pp. 286-287.

[38] Laurence Sterne, *A Sentimental Journey through France and Italy* (London: Oxford University Press, 1928), pp. 218-219.

The little lamb, as I said so,
Frisking about the fields did go,
And, frisking, trod upon my toe.
"Oh!"[39]

"The lambs which sport about you" in Sterne's novel step on your toes in the "real world" of the nursery rhyme and shatter sensibility. It was in this Mother Goose verse that Roethke found the title for his poem "Sensibility! O La!"[40] Just as the nursery rhyme attacks the cult of sensibility in the eighteenth and early nineteenth centuries, Roethke attacks the modern critics who have a limited and thereby limiting concept of sensibility. He presents in his poem a description of a work of art, Botticelli's *The Birth of Venus*, and describes how he, with the delicate (and perhaps artificial) sensitiveness of taste that he finds characteristic of modern sensibility, might respond to it:

In the fair night of some dim brain,
Thou wert marmorean-born.
I name thee: wench of things,
A true zephyr-haunted woodie.
The sea's unequal lengths announced thy birth
From a shell harder than horn.
Thy soft albino gaze
Spoke to my spirit.

(CP 81)

39 William S. Baring-Gould and Ceil Baring-Gould, *The Annotated Mother Goose*, p. 301, no. 809.

40 Roethke could not have come across this poem in *The Annotated Mother Goose* since it was not published until 1962; he found the poem in S. Foster Damon's *William Blake: His Philosophy and Symbols*, p. 41. Damon writes, "The Pastoral had always been one of the great traditions of English verse. From the days of the Elizabethans, it had passed through *Lycidas*, and was to reappear in such a masterpiece as *Adonais*. In the eighteenth century the pastoral had become almost wholly a matter of affectation. Hogarth had expelled it from painting, but the other arts still preserved it. Good old *Mother Goose* thus satirized the popular taste: [text of the nursery rhyme "Dear Sensibility. O la!" follows.]" On the same page of his journal on which Roethke quotes Blake's *Milton* from Damon, he also quotes this nursery rhyme. Theodore Roethke Collection, University of Washington, Seattle (Notebooks, Box 37, #97).

While Roethke responds to the painting, at the same time he makes fun of this response by wryly using words such as "wench" and "woodie," which cannot themselves be identified with a fastidious sensibility.

Botticelli's *Venus* is thought of as one of the great works of the high Renaissance, as an intellectual achievement in which human emotions, including sexual emotions, are refined to an extremely high pitch of sensibility. Roethke asks, Can we develop human passions into sensibilities? Or, if we try to do this, are we thereby associating the wrong function with the wrong animals ("Can a cat milk a hen?")? Are we trying to train our reactions to art in such a way that we violate our natural passions and capabilities? Since Botticelli's painting shows the idealization and apotheosis of a woman, Roethke uses it as a representation of the great historical tradition of woman deified. But the picture speaks not only "to [his] spirit": he wants to extend the range of the definition of sensibility to include not just the capacity for refined taste but also the capacity for physical, even sexual, sensation in response to the aesthetic object:

> Glory to seize, I say. . . .
> John-of-the-thumb's jumping; . . .
> A shape comes to stay:
> The long flesh. . . .
> I'm a twig to touch,
> Pleased as a knife.

The phallic imagery suggests that he wants to bring into his reaction to the woman in the artifact that more basic and passionate sensitivity he would have to a real woman.

In the tradition of sensibility of the type that glorifies Botticelli's *Venus*, exaltation comes as a result of an ever-increasing cultivation of our intellectual responses and a distancing of ourselves from the physical facts of our bodily existence. But for Roethke exaltation can also come, and can come more immediately, from a recognition and acceptance of our interest and inevitable involvement in physicality:

> Exalted? Yes,—
> By the lifting of the tail of a neighbor's
> cat,
> Or that old harpy secreting toads in her
> portmanteau.

The inclusive sensibility that Roethke is finally striving for is not the excessive sentimentality of the eighteenth and early nineteenth centuries, nor the overly dainty sensitivities of those modern minds who can only respond to the intellectual qualities of a work of art, but that defined by T. S. Eliot as possessed by the metaphysical poets of the early seventeenth century—"A mechanism of sensibility which could devour any kind of experience," which could amalgamate "disparate experience."[41] Eliot believed—to quote a famous statement Roethke could not have helped knowing—that "in the seventeenth century a dissociation of sensibility set in, from which we have never recovered." Roethke tries to present in his poems a "unification of sensibility" by bringing together the deified woman (Venus) and the hideous, filthy fallen woman (the "old harpy"). He believes that he has succeeded in combining and responding to "disparate experience": "The shade says: love the sun./I have." His is an integrated sensibility; he has an attitude towards human experience that can encompass and use in poetry both the purified world of Botticelli's intellectual and spiritual sensibility and the real world of flesh, ribs, natural desires, and secretions. By bringing into his poem

[41] T. S. Eliot, "The Metaphysical Poets," *Selected Essays*, p. 247. Roethke was undoubtedly familiar with Eliot's essay since in "On 'Identity'" his definition of a metaphysical poet is taken from Eliot: ". . . an idea for him [the metaphysical poet] can be as real as the smell of a flower." Roethke, "On 'Identity,'" *On the Poet and His Craft*, p. 27. Metaphysical poets "feel their thoughts as immediately as the odour of a rose." Eliot, "The Metaphysical Poets," *Selected Essays*, p. 247.

both the delicate and the indelicate, and by alluding to and making use of many definitions of sensibility as embodied in the literature of several centuries, Roethke in effect strives to meet Eliot's prescription for the modern poet: "Our civilization comprehends great variety and complexity, and this variety and complexity, playing upon a refined sensibility, must produce various and complex results. The poet must become more and more comprehensive, more allusive, more indirect, in order to force, to dislocate if necessary, language into his meaning."[42]

Throughout *Praise to the End!* Roethke uses sounds to reinforce the meaning of his poems. "Give Way, Ye Gates," for example, began with the "caterwauling" of an adolescent;[43] the images were of tough gristle and stiff boards, and the sounds corresponding to the images were equally rough and cacophonous. "O Lull Me, Lull Me," the last poem in Part 1 of the *Praise to the End!* sequence, begins euphoniously: the images of rigidity are replaced by the gentle sighs and breaths intimated by the soft "s" and "f" sounds of the diction. It is appropriate that Roethke unites his sounds in melodious combinations, since this poem belongs to that genre of poetry praising harmony and music, a genre that includes such poems as Milton's "At a Solemn Music" and Dryden's "Alexander's Feast or, The Power of Music." The specific poem from this group that Roethke selects as a source for his title is William Strode's "In Commendation of Musick," which ends

> O lull mee, lull mee, charming ayre,
> My senses rock with wonder sweete;
> Like snowe on wooll thy fallings are,
> Soft, like a spiritts, are thy feete:

42 "The Metaphysical Poets," p. 248.

43 *Botteghe Oscure*, Quaderno No. 6 (1950), p. 449. "I Need, I Need," "Bring the Day!" and "Give Way, Ye Gates" were published in this issue under the one title "GIVE WAY YE GATES." Roethke wrote the following note at the end of the sequence: "I wish to have these three poems considered an entity, the group making one poem from childhood into a violent adolescence: a caterwauling."

Griefe who need feare
That hath an eare?
Down lett him lye
And slumbring dye,
And change his soul for harmony.[44]

According to Strode's stanza, if there is discord and dissension in the soul, music can effect a cure and make the soul harmonious. There is such a lack of concord in Roethke's soul: "I'm crazed and graceless,/A winter-leaping frog" (as opposed, one wonders, to a summersaulting one?). He seeks a state of harmony: "O lull me, lull me" and "Soothe me, great groans of underneath." For Strode, music can bring spiritual peace to the soul since the soul, when it is in its proper state, is in a condition of harmony with itself and with God; and these relationships are musical, or at least can be described only in terms of music. The soul can see within the music an image of its own best self and can imitate that image for its own restoration. Strode achieves harmony by linking his soul with music and with God. Roethke wishes to reach concord by linking the self with the music of nature. The first line is a statement of the situation Roethke wants to consider: "One sigh stretches heaven." There is one huge sigh or rhythmic breathing, one great beat, which is common to all the heavens. Rather than an arrangement of separate harmonies, each individual song is part of one greater harmony, or part of what Strode would probably call the music of the spheres. In the second sentence, Roethke turns his attention to the earth: "In this, the diocese of mice,/Who's bishop of breathing?" Who controls each pulse beat and breath of all the minute creatures of the world? Are they part of this immense harmony? Roethke answers his question by seeing himself as one of these small creatures—a frog. He writes, "I can't go

[44] *The Poetical Works of William Strode*, ed. Bertram Dobell (London: Dobell, 1907), p. 3.

leaping alone." He cannot make up his own harmonies, but has to have a vision of a larger harmony.

For Roethke, however, the harmony need not be consciously arranged music; it can be any rhythmic sound within or without man, from the pulse in his veins to the ebb and flow of the sea ("The beach rises with the waves"). Strode calls for the establishment of harmony within the soul; Roethke wants to bring the beat of the self into harmony with the beat of nature. Roethke concentrates particularly on utterances involving human breath and, to use his implicit metaphor, the breath of nature. One way he not only writes about but also demonstrates the interrelations of man and nature is to use words that refer to these two breaths simultaneously. When he writes, for example, "The air, the air provides," he refers both to Strode's "charming ayre" and to that which we breathe. Each stanza in Strode's poem is a carefully constructed conceit through which man, God, and music are linked in harmony. Roethke's poem clearly does not have these extended comparisons: the conceit has been abandoned in favor of individual words that themselves link together man, nature, and music. Many of Roethke's words, like those very creatures he mentions in his poem (otter, snail, frog), are in this sense amphibious.

At the end of the poem the protagonist has a vision of the great natural harmony, but we are still left in doubt as to whether or not he has actually joined in the song. In fact, just before the concluding lines, Roethke stresses that he remains in a state of anticipation: "I'm still waiting for a foot./The poke of the wind's close." As a "frog," he is waiting for a prod from a person's foot. As a poet, he is waiting for a metrical foot, for a rhythm. Roethke's play on words was probably suggested by the line, "Soft, like a spiritts, are thy feete," in which Strode refers both to the feet of spirits and to the divisions of verse in the "ayre." As the last stanza of Roethke's poem proceeds, the protagonist moves nearer and nearer to joining the harmony:

I'm all ready to whistle; . . .
I could say hello to things;
I could talk to a snail.

But "*could* say hello" and "*could* talk," while expressing his ability to greet and respond to nature, also suggest a shade of doubt. Still, Roethke at least has what he as a potential singer must have just before joining into the song fully—a clear perception of the harmony: "I see what sings!/What sings!"

Praise to the End! moves boldly through the stages of man's ever-changing relationships with nature as he grows from infancy to adulthood. We begin with the unified natural sensibility of the child, but inevitably the dissociation between the child and his environment sets in. With "Bring the Day!" and "Give Way, Ye Gates," Roethke begins an attempt to reintegrate physicality into the adult consciousness. In the next poem we are confronted with an investigation of how that unification may be wrought—at least within the context of poetic sensibilities. This pattern of changing self-awareness is consistently linked with the rhythms (or dissonances) of nature through the imagery of the poems. In the final poem, "O Lull Me, Lull Me," harmony itself rather than what is harmonized becomes the central consideration. The necessary pre-condition for this journey from unity to division to re-unification is the widening of Roethke's own sensibilities to construct and encompass a literary tradition characterized by similar cycles of self and other.

IV

Archetypes of Tradition

Sooner or later in almost every lengthy study of Theodore Roethke the name C. G. Jung appears. At first he is introduced tentatively with footnotes explaining that "the precise extent and nature" of Roethke's reading in his works is "not certain"; or that Roethke's poetry is linked with Jung's theories—but only as they are mediated through his exegete, Maud Bodkin, with whose *Archetypal Patterns in Poetry* Roethke was familiar. Before long, however, that which was suggested as provisional is considered proved: caution and Bodkin are flung to the winds, and Jung is firmly established as a direct influence upon Roethke.[1] But in a study of Roethke's poetry it is most important to maintain the distinctions between Jung's and Bodkin's inquiries and to keep Bodkin as an intercessor between the psychologist and the poet.[2]

The Jungian archetypes in Roethke's poetry were transmitted to him through Bodkin's literary study, and refer primarily to psychological patterns found in literature and only secondarily—or, to be more precise, only through the medium of a literary tradition—to theories about the human psyche. When Roethke wishes to bring into his poetry

[1] See Karl Malkoff, *Theodore Roethke*, p. 59, and Stanley Kunitz, "Roethke: Poet of Transformations," *New Republic*, No. 152 (January 23, 1965), p. 25. All further quotations from Kunitz are from this page. Malkoff's first few references to Jung are in connection with Maud Bodkin; in the next dozen references, he implicitly assumes that Jung is a direct influence.

[2] See C. G. Jung, *Contributions to Analytical Psychology*, trans. H. G. and Cary F. Baynes (London: Kegan Paul, 1928) and Maud Bodkin, *Archetypal Patterns in Poetry: Psychological Studies of Imagination* (London: Oxford University Press, 1934).

some Jungian perspective on the human mind, he does so by evoking certain literary modes, which are, in Bodkin's theories, the most readily available embodiments of the often unrecognized patterns of human psychology. His poems are neither versified psychology nor versified literary theory, but rather new variations upon and extensions of those literary motifs which Jung and principally Bodkin singled out as products of the archetypes of the human mind. Finally, Bodkin's theories have an even more important function than as a reservoir of images, for in the idea of the archetype Roethke found a concept of tradition allowing him to respond to and bring into his mature poetry a host of poets and poems that made use of the particular archetype he wished to employ. For Roethke, Jung and Bodkin were less significant as explorers of the human mind than as discoverers of a means for organizing the past so that it stimulates creation in the present.

Roethke wrote that each of the poems in the second part of *Praise to the End!* (in which "The Lost Son" appeared in 1951) is "complete in itself; yet each in a sense is a stage in a kind of struggle out of the slime; part of a slow spiritual progress; an effort to be born, and later, to become something more." The process of these poems is "cyclic": "I believe that to go forward as a spiritual man it is necessary first to go back. Any history of the psyche (or allegorical journey) is bound to be a succession of experiences, similar yet dissimilar. There is a perpetual slipping-back, then a going-forward; but there is some 'progress.' . . . Some of these pieces, then, begin in the mire."[3]

Stanley Kunitz was the first to point out that these passages fused together "point straight to the door of Dr. Jung or to the door of Jung's disciple Maud Bodkin" and their archetype of progression and regression. But Roethke's comments about "regression" and "return" in connection with his remarks about the protagonist of "The Lost Son"

[3] "Open Letter," *On the Poet and His Craft*, pp. 37, 39-40.

"hunting, like a primitive, for some animistic suggestion, some clue to existence from the sub-human"[4] lead also to another door—that of T. S. Eliot and his definition of the "auditory imagination": "What I call the 'auditory imagination' is the feeling for syllable and rhythm, penetrating far below the conscious levels of thought and feeling, invigorating every word; sinking to the most primitive and forgotten, returning to the origin and bringing something back, seeking the beginning and the end. It works through meanings, certainly, or not without meanings in the ordinary sense, and fuses the old and obliterated and the trite, the current, and the new and surprising, the most ancient and the most civilised mentality."[5]

We can be certain that this passage from Eliot was well-known to Roethke: he owned *The Use of Poetry and the Use of Criticism* in which the passage occurs,[6] and, more importantly, in his essay "Some Remarks on Rhythm," he himself defined "what Eliot has called 'the auditory imagination' " as "the sinuousness, a rhythm like the tail of a fish" and as the "primitiveness of the imagination."[7] His remarks are particularly interesting when we remember that he described the protagonist of "The Lost Son" as "a primitive" searching for clues that "he sees and yet does not see," that "are almost tail-flicks, from another world" ("Open Letter," p. 38). Roethke's poetry is often as much directed by rhythmical patterns (suggested by Eliot's concept of the

[4] "Open Letter," p. 38. Roethke uses the words "regression" and "return" in a letter describing the pattern of "The Shape of the Fire," *Selected Letters*, p. 142.

[5] T. S. Eliot, *The Use of Poetry and the Use of Criticism: Studies in the Relation of Criticism to Poetry in England* (London: Faber and Faber, 1933), pp. 118-119.

[6] See "Annotated Volumes in the Theodore Roethke Collection," an unpublished list compiled by the University of Washington Library.

[7] "Some Remarks on Rhythm," *On the Poet and His Craft*, pp. 80-81.

auditory imagination) as it is controlled by an adherence to image patterns (suggested by Jungian psychology).[8]

In the same essay in which Eliot describes the auditory imagination, he comments upon Matthew Arnold's famous pronouncement that "Poetry is at bottom a criticism of life." Eliot answers, "At bottom: that is a great way down; the bottom is the bottom. At the bottom of the abyss is what few ever see, and what those cannot bear to look at for long; and it is not a 'criticism of life'" (p. 111). Roethke's conception of the poetic experience is similar to Eliot's, and he too uses the metaphor of the pit: "To begin from the depths and come out—that is difficult; for few know where the depths are or can recognize them; or, if they do, are afraid" ("Open Letter," p. 40). Roethke may also have acquired his idea of progression through regression from Eliot's line in *Four Quartets*, "the way forward is the way back," one of the more succinct statements of a theme that runs repeatedly throughout Eliot's poetry and plays. Since in the last section of "The Lost Son," Roethke again turns to the *Four Quartets* as a source for ideas and even images, it once more seems likely that the literary center from which his poetry flows is other poetry, rather than abstract psychological treatises.

The title of the first poem in Part II of *Praise to the End!*, unlike the titles in Part I, has no specific source. Instead "The Lost Son" is an extensively referential title, suggesting a character type that recurs throughout poetry. The lost son is not only Roethke himself but also an image that refers to those many examples of the archetype of the lost son, including, to name just a few, Telemachus, Oedipus, Orestes, Aeneas, Hamlet, and Blake's "Little Boy lost." Roethke's titles for the various sections of his poem—such as "The Flight," "The Pit," and "The Return"—suggest the most

[8] In his conversations about poetry (both his own and that written by others), Roethke would not begin by pointing out the themes or intellectual content of the images in a line, but would first seize upon its rhythm and sound effects.

basic archetype in literature, the death-rebirth theme. Character and sequence of action are combined to embody other archetypal patterns: Roethke's "lost son" descending into "the pit" recalls, for instance, Aeneas journeying to the underworld to find his father, Hamlet leaping into the "clay pit" that is Ophelia's grave, Satan falling into the bottomless pit, and Blake's "Little Boy lost" wandering in the deep mire. Roethke's working conception of a literary tradition has become even broader than the relationships established through the titles in Part I of *Praise to the End!* The Jung-Bodkin theories of archetypal patterns in literature unify Roethke's conception of a literary tradition, because instead of an omnium-gatherum of different poets, each with his own style and themes, the poets in his tradition are now all linked together through the perception of archetypes appearing in much of the work of each poet. The resulting historical conception of poetry is in these ways similar to Northrop Frye's unification of literature by means of archetypal patterns in the *Anatomy of Criticism.*

The literary background of the archetypes in "The Lost Son" is extensive; tracing any one of these major patterns through the literature with which Roethke was familiar would take many pages of commentary, but by following the development of a single image in the poem and determining its background, the processes by which Roethke transformed his experience of literature into his own poetry can be illuminated. Although it is certainly not one of Bodkin's major archetypal patterns, the image of "slime" that Roethke uses in several poems lends itself well to such a study. In his poem "Slug," he emphasizes lubricity through the repeated *sl*-sound: "When I slip, just slightly, in the dark,/I know it isn't a wet leaf,/But you, loose toe from the old life,/The cold slime come into being . . . /Creeping slowly over the wet grass." In "The Lost Son," he uses words such as "sleek," "slime," "slither," "slept," "slippery," and images suggesting unpleasant dampness and moisture: "Toads brooding in wells./All the leaves stuck out their tongues." Bodkin points out that in Coleridge's "The Rime of the Ancient Mariner" the "slimy things" that "did crawl with legs/Upon the slimy sea" were of an ambivalent character. The Mariner, she writes, "first despised and then accepted with love [these slimy creatures], to his own salvation. Before 'a renewal of life' can come about, Jung urges, there must be an acceptance of the possibilities that lie in the unconscious contents 'activated through regression . . . and disfigured by the slime of the deep' " (p. 52). Like the Mariner, the protagonist in Roethke's poem realizes that the slime contains not only "objectionable animal tendencies, but also germs of new possibilities of life," and thus he entreats, "Snail, snail, glister me forward." Just as the Mariner finally stops despising the "thousand, thousand slimy things" and sees their radiance, sees that "they moved in tracks of shining white,/ . . . and every track/Was a flash of golden fire,"[9] Roethke sees the slime the snail leaves on its track not as repugnant and viscous but as a brilliant substance that "glisters"—glitters and gleams.

The Mariner's realization of the slimy creatures' beauty breaks the spell that has been upon him: he can now "pray." At the end of the poem, he reflects upon this experience and formulates that

> He prayeth best, who loveth best
> All things both great and small;
> For the dear God who loveth us,
> He made and loveth all.

Similarly, Roethke writes, "Everything that lives is holy: I call upon these holy forms of life. One could even put this theologically: St. Thomas says, 'God is above all things by the excellence of His nature; nevertheless, He is in all things as causing the being of all things.' Therefore, in calling upon the snail [in 'The Lost Son'], I am calling, in a sense,

[9] *The Poems of Samuel Taylor Coleridge*, ed. Ernest Hartley Coleridge (London: Oxford University Press, 1912), p. 198. All further quotations from Coleridge's poems are from this edition.

upon God."[10] When the Mariner, surrounded by dead bodies, is able to pray, "the ship moves on." When Roethke, in the cemetery, calls upon God, he too begins to move "forward." But for Roethke, as we have seen, to go forward involves first going back, and thus he begins his slow journey by exploring his past:

> Fished in an old wound,
> The soft pond of repose;
> Nothing nibbled my line,
> Not even the minnows came.
> (CP 53)

Roethke continues to use images suggesting slime: the old wound is an open one that has never healed, like a stagnant pond of standing water. In his poem "The Minimal," lice, squirmers, and bacterial creepers go "Wriggling through wounds/Like elvers in ponds, . . . /Cleaning and caressing,/ Creeping and healing" (CP 50). But in this "wound," or "soft pond," there is no movement at all. Instead, Roethke gives expression to the state of "soul-sickness" through images of "foul and stagnant water—the water of meres and marshes," as do both Coleridge and Emile Verhaeren.[11] He fishes in the dark pond of his private memory and of his memory of literature, particularly as it is distilled by Bodkin.

The desire for motion leads the lost son to demand: "Tell me:/Which is the way I take?"

> Dark hollows said, lee to the wind,
> The moon said, back of an eel.

(Notice how for Roethke not only is "the way forward the way back," but also the word forward is the word back-

[10] "On 'Identity,'" *On the Poet and His Craft*, pp. 24-25. Although Roethke does not put "Everything that lives is holy" in quotation marks, it is a direct quotation from Blake's *Visions of the Daughters of Albion* (from which Roethke took his title "I Cry, Love! Love!") and from *The Four Zoas* and *The Marriage of Heaven and Hell*, to which Roethke later in "The Lost Son" turns for images and a diction.

[11] Bodkin, p. 49.

wards, "eel" being the reverse of "lee.") "Back of an eel" suggests another image of slime. Since the path of possible regeneration is once more shown to lie in the glutinous mud, the protagonist goes "running lightly over spongy ground":

> Hunting along the river,
> Down among the rubbish, the bug-riddled
> foliage,
> By the muddy pond-edge, by the bog-holes,
> By the shrunken lake, hunting, in the heat of
> summer.

"Those places, holes, and slippery mud patches," Ralph J. Mills, Jr. writes, ". . . spell out the dangers of regression and defeat to his odyssey."[12] On the contrary, it is as we have seen only amid the slime that the lost son can hope to find a possibility of being renewed. He is "hunting for some clue to existence from the sub-human"—he is "hunting for chinks in the dark," like the bulbs in "that cellar, dank as a ditch" ("Root Cellar," CP 38).

All the various images of slimy cavities in the ground ("wells," "the soft pond," "the bog-holes," "the shrunken lake") lead up to "The Pit" in part 2 of the poem, which is described as an oozy breeding place: "I feel the slime of a wet nest." The protagonist's regressive quest has resulted in vaginal and womb imagery. This pit down under the roots also presents a vision of the underworld, and, in a study of archetypes, the lost son's plunge into the abyss could be compared to Aeneas' descent into Hades, Dante's journey to Hell, or even Jonah's entry into the whale's belly, which is described in the Bible as a descent beneath the earth ("The depth closed me round about, the weeds were wrapped about my head. I went down to the bottoms of the mountains; the earth with her bars was about me for ever" 2:5,6). But Roethke particularizes his use of the pit metaphor by placing it within a specific context that directs

[12] Ralph J. Mills, Jr., *Theodore Roethke*, p. 25.

us to Blake's *The Book of Thel.* "Thel's Motto" begins, "Does the Eagle know what is in the pit?/Or wilt thou go ask the Mole?" Roethke writes in "The Pit," "Where do the roots go?/ . . . Ask the mole, he knows."

There are many different interpretations of "Thel's Motto," but the one that seems to have influenced Roethke when he wrote "The Lost Son" is Emily S. Hamblen's in *On the Minor Prophecies of William Blake* (1930), a book Roethke owned.[13] *A Blake Bibliography* reports that "Miss Hamblen had two unusual advantages in writing her book: she had 'deliberately avoided reading any of those recent writers who also have attempted a complete inquiry [into Blake],' and she had been assisted by visitations from the dead." "The result," the editors of the bibliography wryly observe, "is everything that might be expected."[14] Roethke would not, of course, have been deterred by these characteristics of Hamblen's work, since he too on occasion felt that "they—the poets dead—were with [him]."[15] Besides, Hamblen's analysis of the "Motto" seems fairly reasonable: "The meaning [of the motto] is clear. Where will one go for knowledge? To him [the eagle] through whom no revelation by reason of his peculiar nature can be given, or to him [the mole] who through his very typical reactions will have understanding?" The region of the subconscious, she continues, belongs to the mole: "In very ancient literature the rodents stand for the instincts. Observe also Nietzsche's use of the symbol when he speaks of himself as an 'old mole-hunter and rat-catcher.' Thel, wishing to learn of the hidden motives and impulses which, though covered, are active in human thought and conduct, will not look to

[13] See "Annotated Volumes in the Books Shipped from Saginaw," part of an unpublished list of Roethke's books compiled by the University of Washington Library.

[14] *A Blake Bibliography*, ed. G. E. Bentley, Jr. and Martin K. Nurmi (Minneapolis: University of Minnesota Press, 1964), p. 280, no. 1307.

[15] "On 'Identity,'" p. 24.

the sublime expressions of man's soul but will interrogate his earthly nature."[16]

Like Hamblen's Nietzsche, the protagonist of "The Lost Son" is a "mole hunter and rat-catcher": it is rodents he is "hunting along the river, . . . hunting, in the heat of summer." Particularly, the lost son is searching for the mole, that creature "soft like a mouse," "sleek as an otter," and bigger than "the shape of a rat." When he is unable to find the mole "by the muddy pond-edge" or "by the shrunken lake," he plunges into the depths of the pit himself, into the region of the subconscious, to gain knowledge of the hidden.

By quoting from *The Book of Thel*, Roethke suggests that he is descending into Blake's poetry as well as into the pit: he is inquiring into the relationship between himself and earlier poets and into the ways in which a search into one's subconscious can be facilitated by a knowledge of previous explorations. At the beginning of "The Gibber," the section immediately following "The Pit," Roethke again refers to Blake when he writes,

> At the wood's mouth,
> By the cave's door,
> I listened to something
> I had heard before.

This passage echoes Blake's allegory of the "cave's mouth" in *The Marriage of Heaven and Hell*,[17] describing "the method in which knowledge is transmitted from generation to generation." Roethke indeed listens to something he has heard before—in Blake's poetry. Through an approach

[16] Emily S. Hamblen, *On the Minor Prophecies of William Blake* (London: Dent, 1930), pp. 146-147.

[17] Roethke also alludes to *The Marriage of Heaven and Hell* in "The Long Alley," the poem following "The Lost Son" in *The Collected Poems*, when he writes, "The soul resides in the horse barn," "Nuts are money," and other enigmatic sayings structured like Blake's "Proverbs of Hell": "The tygers of wrath are wiser than the horses of instruction," "Exuberance is Beauty," etc.

to literature characterized by the discovery of archetypal patterns, he demonstrates that the knowledge in the poetry of a past generation can be transmitted to his own. As he writes, "the dead," and he means explicitly dead poets, "can come to our aid in a quest for identity."[18]

In that section of "The Gibber" described by Roethke as "rendered in terms of balked sexual experience," images of slime reappear in the form of semen and saliva:

From the mouths of jugs
Perched on many shelves,
I saw substance flowing
That cold morning.

Like a slither of eels
That watery cheek
As my own tongue kissed
My lips awake.

The passage before these two stanzas images a state of repose, or, as Roethke defines it, "a crooning serenity." The passage directly following them is a violent "rant" ("Is this the storm's heart?") ("Open Letter," p. 38). This shift from calm to storm and the imagery of the intervening stanzas in Roethke's poem basically parallel the movement and imagery in Coleridge's "The Ancient Mariner." "Before the description of the outburst of activity in the elements [i.e., a storm]," Bodkin writes, "there comes a moment of true and blissful quiescence: 'Oh sleep! it is a gentle thing.' " "In Coleridge's poem the relief of rain follows the relaxing of the inner tension by the act of love and prayer . . .":[19]

The silly buckets on the deck,
That had so long remained,
I dreamt that they were filled with dew;
And when I awoke, it rained.

[18] "On 'Identity,' " p. 24.
[19] Bodkin, pp. 69 and 48.

My lips were wet, my throat was cold,
My garments all were dank;
Sure I had drunken in my dreams,
And still my body drank.

The last two sections of "The Lost Son" present a movement from the pit to the greenhouse, from darkness to light, and from lost to found. Accordingly, the images of slime disappear or, more accurately, are purified. The viscid substances secreted by the human body in the first part of "The Gibber" are changed into more fluid liquids—"primordial milk" and "water." These watery liquids are converted into "white snow" and "steam." The snow, in turn, becomes "frost" melting away, and the steam "a fine haze" moving off the leaves. These images finally culminate in the last section of the poem in "the clear air."

To understand why Roethke made such great use of Blake and Coleridge, it is necessary to view "The Lost Son" as a poem "about a mental and spiritual crisis."[20] Novelist Allan Seager ends an early chapter in his biography of Roethke by writing that "His history, as he [Roethke] saw it, was one of losses, betrayals, shame, many fears, and guilt. To immerse himself in these, to force them into images or to contemplate them until they became images that he, hence others, could accept, and to find a suitable diction for them was not only taxing but may have been dangerous."[21] This rather frightening statement is only a conjecture, but Roethke's poetry does seem to bear it out. The periodic mental breakdowns he was liable to during every part of his adult life were a part of his history that he tried to "find a suitable diction for" and to give objective form to in his poetry. His early poems about his mental illness deal with it wittily, as if he could objectify the experience and detach himself from it only by treating it with humor. In two early

20 *Selected Letters*, p. 114 (letter of February 27, 1945).

21 Allan Seager, *The Glass House: The Life of Theodore Roethke* (New York: McGraw-Hill, 1968), p. 85.

poems published in 1937, "Meditation in Hydrotherapy" and "Lines upon Leaving a Sanitarium" (CP 256, 257), he straitjackets the violence of his first breakdown by binding it in closed, balanced octosyllabic couplets. He has not yet found a proper diction for his despair and, rather than coming to terms with it, he removes himself from the experience by intellectualizing it through iambic tetrameter and abstractions, employing expressions such as "primal element," "self-contemplation," "old confusion," "mental ill," "recumbency," and "dissection."

Roethke was not able to transmute his "madness" into poetry successfully until he viewed himself as belonging to the tradition of mad poets in whom the extraordinary capacity for imaginative creation is linked with insanity.[22] In "Heard in a Violent Ward," he sees himself as placed in an asylum with the other so-called "mad" poets:

> In heaven, too,
> You'd be institutionalized.
> But that's all right,—
> If they let you eat and swear
> With the likes of Blake,
> And Christopher Smart,
> And that sweet man, John Clare.
> (CP 228)[23]

The colloquial tone, the epithet of endearment ("that sweet man"), and the image of eating and blaspheming together make the four poets appear to be close and contemporary acquaintances, as if Roethke's statement were similar to Dr.

[22] This idea was first suggested to me by Stanley Kunitz in a conversation on December 28, 1968.

[23] Yeats invokes the same literary "madness" in "An Acre of Grass":

> Grant me an old man's frenzy,
> Myself must I remake
> Till I am Timon and Lear
> Or that William Blake
> Who beat upon the wall
> Till Truth obeyed his call.

Johnson's, "I'd as lief pray with Kit Smart as with any man." Although it is only in this poem that Roethke explicitly states that he considers himself as one of the group of "mad" poets, in other poems such as "The Lost Son" we find him struggling to learn the techniques of those writers so that he, like them, can translate his mental state (whether mad or divinely inspired) into poetry.

Roethke usually tried to write his poetry as a result of actual personal experience and his experience of literature: when he wished to write poems about his experiences of nature as a boy, he turned to Wordsworth, the poet of nature. Now, in "The Lost Son" and the other long poems of his second book, the immediate personal experience out of which he must mold his poetry is a mental collapse serious enough to require hospitalization. Accordingly he turns to Blake, a poet whom he considered to have a vocabulary capable of expressing (and perhaps thereby controlling) madness. Roethke found the diction with which to represent his breakdown in Night the First of *The Four Zoas*, a poem that as a whole and in each of its parts presents the "breakdown" of the giant Albion, who in his fall shatters into pieces, each fragment being one of the Four Zoas. Unlike the abstract constructions in "Meditation in Hydrotherapy" and "Lines upon Leaving a Sanitarium," the vocabulary of "The Lost Son" is concrete, denoting "things" rather than qualities and states. When choosing his words from Blake's poem, Roethke avoided the indefinite nominals and abstruse mythological names. He saw something in Blake that few before had noticed: he saw that Blake's strength as a poet lay not in making up names nor in forming vague nouns from verbs, but in investing simple nouns and familiar verbs with evocative value. It is this part of Blake's vocabulary that Roethke found congenial to his own purposes and he therefore borrowed in order to communicate his own ideas about madness.[24]

24 "The Lost Son" has over 160 words in common with Night the First of *The Four Zoas*, including "lost," "son," "lulled," "iron,"

Roethke also found the basic movement of Night the First commensurate with his own formal intentions for "The Lost Son." The beginning book of *The Four Zoas* is one of Blake's many summations of the whole process of the fall from primal unity into division, followed by a restoration to a higher unity. "The plot" [of Night the First], S. Foster Damon writes, "begins with the first signs of the Fall into Experience: the Body is losing its exultation in life, and is out of communication with the Earth Mother."[25] This is an accurate description of the protagonist's condition at the start of "The Lost Son": his body is losing its delight in life ("I shook the softening chalk of my bones"), and he too is out of communication with Nature ("Voice, come out of the silence./Say something.") But, rather than tracing the movement of Roethke's poem through all Nine Nights of *The Four Zoas*, we can find an epitome of the same process of the descent into experience and the return to a higher state of innocence in Blake's "lost" and "found" lyrics:

The Little Boy lost

"Father! father! where are you going?
"O do not walk so fast.
"Speak, father, speak to your little boy,
"Or else I shall be lost."

The night was dark, no father was there;
The child was wet with dew;
The mire was deep, & the child did weep,
And away the vapour flew.

"brooding," "bones," "wound," "shadows," "one fly," "spider," "kingdom," "webby" (from Blake's "web"), "roots," "Mother," "cave," "howl," "Fear," "Father," "veins," "stalk," and "bloody."

[25] S. Foster Damon, *William Blake: His Philosophy and Symbols*, p. 156.

The Little Boy found

The little boy lost in the lonely fen,
Led by the wand'ring light,
Began to cry; but God, ever nigh,
Appear'd like his father in white . . .

In addition to the obvious similarities between the titles, there are other fundamental parallels between Blake's poems and Roethke's. For both poets, the physical condition of the little boy lost in the Stygian darkness and trapped in the mire is an emblem for a state of psychological disorientation and for a loss of the true vision of innocence. The restoration to innocence comes about for the lost sons through the appearance of a divine father-figure who illuminates the dark world. As Roethke writes about "The Return," "after the dark night, the morning brings with it the suggestion of a renewing light: a coming of 'Papa.' . . . the papa on earth and heaven are blended" ("Open Letter," pp. 38-39).

Another work of Blake's in which Roethke found ideas compatible with his own is *The Book of Thel.* In "Thel's Motto," Blake shows the necessity for descending into experience; Roethke, by referring to the motto through the phrase "ask the mole" in "The Pit," also stresses the importance of going down into the pit of madness, chaos, and disorder, and returning from it. *The Book of Thel*, however, ends where "The Lost Son" begins. Thel looks into the depths, hears the "voice of sorrow breathed from the hollow pit," is terrified, and flees back to her state of inoperative innocence. Roethke's poem opens with a similar "flight": "a terrified running away—with alternate periods of hallucinatory waiting (the voices, etc.)" ("Open Letter," p. 38). But, unlike Thel, the lost son finally goes into the abyss of experience and returns to a state of enlightened innocence. Although Thel's is a broken quest, while the lost son's probe is finally concluded, both protagonists in their searching make similar inquiries: Thel asks, "Art thou but a Worm?"

and "Dost thou, O little Cloud?"; the lost son queries, "Has the worm a shadow?/What do the clouds say?" Both are asking questions about human experience. When Thel hears the answers, she withdraws; whereas Roethke's protagonist can accept the answers, come to terms with them, and thus pass through the pit into illumination. Roethke is able to make use of *The Four Zoas*, "The Little Boy lost," "The Little Boy found," and *The Book of Thel* because he can discover and bring into his own work the underlying archetypal patterns of innocence and experience, of being lost and found, of dissolution and unity, that are basic to Blake's thought.

Like Blake's long poems and Coleridge's "The Ancient Mariner," "The Lost Son" is "dramatic" poetry as Roethke defines it—"with the mood or the action on the page, not talked-about, not the meditative, T. S. Eliot kind of thing."[26] For Roethke believes that "in this kind of poem, the poet should not 'comment,' or use many judgment-words; instead he should render the experience, however condensed or elliptical that experience may be. (That's what has happened to Eliot in the *Quartets*. His rhythms are weakened; there's too much talk. It's a reflective, not a dramatic poetry.) You watch: What I say is true."[27] In the final section of "The Lost Son," however, Roethke wants to establish a "meditative" and "reflective" mood to communicate his quiet, tranquil state of illumination, and thus he turns to Eliot for assistance. Like a soliloquy in a play, the contemplative passage at the end of Roethke's poem is, of course, part of the larger drama of the whole poem, and finally must be viewed in this dramatic context, rather than as an isolated meditation.

Several critics have suggested that the last part of Roethke's poem recalls Eliot's style. "At the end," Roy Harvey Pearce writes, "there is a recollection of 'Ash-Wednesday.' "[28] According to Karl Malkoff, "many critics have

[26] *Selected Letters*, p. 122. [27] *Selected Letters*, p. 142.

[28] Roy Harvey Pearce, "Theodore Roethke: The Power of Sympathy," *Theodore Roethke: Essays on the Poetry*, ed. Stein, p. 184.

seen in these lines a direct allusion to Eliot's 'still point of the turning world' ('Burnt Norton')." "Their case is strengthened," he adds, "by the similarity of the beginning of the fifth section to the opening lines of 'Little Gidding' " (p. 90). These critics are quite right in directing the reader to Eliot, but they have not pointed to the exact passage Roethke consciously chose to imitate and upon which he played his own variations. Rather than the first poem ("Burnt Norton") or the last ("Little Gidding"), he selected "East Coker," one of the two in-between poems of the *Four Quartets*, as the immediate exemplar on which to pattern the description of his own "in-between time," as can be seen by comparing the first two stanzas of Eliot's poem with Roethke's:

> In my beginning is my end. . . .
> Bone of . . . cornstalk and leaf. . . .
> And a time for the wind. . . .
>
> In my beginning is my end. Now the light falls
> Across the open field,
> . . . . in the empty silence.
> ("East Coker," Part I)

> It was beginning winter,
> An in-between time, . . .
> The bones of weeds kept swinging in the wind. . . .
>
> It was beginning winter,
> The light moved slowly over the frozen field, . . .
> Light traveled over the wide field;
> . . . . in the silence.
> ("The Lost Son," Part 5)

Not only does Roethke adopt Eliot's vocabulary, but also he uses the words "beginning," "bone," "wind," "beginning," "light," "field," and "silence" in the same order. Both poets are attempting to set forth a period of time between two events, actions, or states: in Part III of "East Coker," Eliot presents images of an underground train stopping between stations, a darkened theatre between scenes, and a mind suspended under ether; Roethke simply states, "It was . . . /An in-between time." But for Eliot this halted interval is a metaphor to describe the permanent condition of life with which he must come to terms; whereas for Roethke it is only a temporary condition. The basic movement of "East Coker" is from a positive consideration of the cycles of life (death and renewal) to a rejection of the knowledge of these cycles as either a means for the development of a morality or a means for writing poems, and finally to a stoical acceptance of a negative stance from which to develop a system of thought and poetry. Roethke begins with the cycles of nature—and, instead of rejecting them, accepts them. He brings into his own poem (at the start of Part 5) the suggestion of an interim typical of Eliot, particularly Eliot in "East Coker," but he has a very different response to it: he believes that after suspended animation there will be re-animation, a restoration to light. Eliot writes that waiting is continual—a waiting based on hopelessness; Roethke writes that waiting is conditional—a waiting with hope for regeneration. Compare the poets' exhortations to their souls:

> I said to my soul, be still and wait without hope.
> ("East Coker," Part III)

> A lively understandable spirit
> Once entertained you.
> It will come again.
> Be still.
> Wait.
> ("The Lost Son," Part 5)

As Roy Harvey Pearce suggests, "The Lost Son" "constitutes a kind of reply to Eliot, or an alternative."[29]

One of the strongest links between the two poems is the contrast between Eliot's darkness and Roethke's light. Eliot's fourfold cry, "O dark dark dark. They all go into the dark," becomes in Roethke

[29] Pearce, p. 184.

Was it light?
Was it light within?
Was it light within light?

The pattern of Roethke's questions suggests an intensification rather than the diminution expressed in Eliot's similar construction from "The Waste Land": "What are you thinking of? What thinking? What?" Eliot's lines, "I said to my soul, be still, and let the dark come upon you/Which shall be the darkness of God," suggest that he has turned to traditional forms of negative mysticism, more or less in the Christian tradition. Roethke's metaphors continue to be based upon archetypal patterns rooted in the natural world and experienced through the poetry of his tradition, rather than on the mystical transcendence of the natural. He does not turn towards theological systems, but remains in the hope of personal, direct illumination—like his father's "roses" that "kept breathing in the dark," and when "the morning came . . . turned toward the light."

"The Lost Son" first appeared in 1947, some four years before publication of *Praise to the End!* Yet when Roethke established the sequence of poems in his third volume, he reprinted the earlier poem following the newer ones. In "The Lost Son" Roethke creates for himself a tradition by joining together diverse poets sharing similar motifs. His method, guided by the archetypal studies of Bodkin, is at once both more rigorous and more stimulating than the loose associations underlying the allusive titles in Part I of *Praise to the End!* The sequence of the poems records not the chronology of their composition, but the development of Roethke's sense of a tradition that, in retrospect, he saw occurring in his poems. The volume itself demonstrates one of its central themes—"to go forward as a spiritual man it is necessary first to go back."

V

A Motion Not His Own

As Roethke nears the end of his "sequence of dramatic pieces beginning with a small child and working up,"[1] he looks back over what he has done: thus the images in "Unfold! Unfold!" rather than alluding only to Henry Vaughan's brief poem "The Revival" from which Roethke took his title, also refer back to the previous poems in the sequence. Roethke "revives" many of his most characteristic images and "unfolds" what his methods in writing the long poems have been. In the first line, for example, he cites rather than uses some of those images which are central in the development of the earlier poems of the sequence: "By snails, by leaps of frog, I came here . . ." (CP 89). It is as though he were at once expounding and summarizing his method.

Kenneth Burke, in his pioneering essay, "The Vegetal Radicalism of Theodore Roethke," writes that the poet " 'regressed' as thoroughly as he could, even at considerable risk, toward a language of sheer 'intuition' . . . his search for essential motives has driven him back into the quandaries of adolescence, childhood, even infancy."[2] Although Roethke

[1] *Selected Letters of Theodore Roethke*, p. 148.

[2] Kenneth Burke, "The Vegetal Radicalism of Theodore Roethke," *Language as Symbolic Action: Essays on Life, Literature, and Method* (Berkeley: University of California Press, 1968), pp. 277, 278. This essay was originally published in the *Sewanee Review*, No. 58 (1950). Before he had read Burke's essay in its entirety on September 17, 1949, Roethke was obviously familiar with parts of it (see, for example, his letter to Burke, ca. March 1946). He is probably referring to Burke's essay when he writes in a letter to Burke on September 6, 1949, "I wouldn't be surprised if I find I've taken up, by metaphorical indirection or ironical aside, one or two of the points you make in the Great Screed" (*Selected Letters*, pp. 155-156).

in a letter to Burke does not altogether accept this statement (". . . by back I mean down into the consciousness of the race itself not just the quandries [sic] of adolescence, damn it"),[3] in "Unfold! Unfold!" he evaluates his own long poems in metaphorical language consonant with Burke's description: "The last time I nearly whispered myself away./I was far back, farther than anybody else." Roethke knows too that he must extend his vision to include other modes if he is to develop: "The eye perishes in the small vision" and "The single vision becomes a shade, a shutter, a trap," he writes,[4] recalling Blake's "May God us keep/From single vision & Newton's sleep!"

Vaughan wrote in "The Retreat,"

> Happy those early days! When I
> Shin'd in my angel-infancy. . . .
> O how I long to travel back
> And tread again that ancient track![5]

Roethke in his series of long poems did "retreat" into his "infancy," but now he is ready to start exploring another phase of life: "I can't crawl back through those veins,/I ache for another choice." One reason he can no longer dig into "those veins" is that they have already been completely mined. In "The Revival," Vaughan wrote, "Hark how his winds have chang'd their note." Referring to this poem through his title, Roethke in effect suggests that he longs for a similar revival. What his new "note" will be, he does not say, but he does realize that "It's a soul's crossing time." "There are now eight pieces in all in the sequence; maybe

[3] *Selected Letters*, p. 116.

[4] The first quotation is from "Unfold! Unfold!" The second is from one of Roethke's notebooks. Theodore Roethke Collection, University of Washington, Seattle (Notebooks, Box 37, #267). "Notebook #267 has been identified by David Wagoner as 1948 and has been placed in chronological sequence after notebook #99."

[5] *The Complete Poetry of Henry Vaughan*, ed. French Fogle (New York: Anchor, 1964), p. 169. All subsequent quotations from Vaughan are from this edition.

one more kid's one," he wrote in a letter to Burke in 1949. "The last two are called *Unfold! Unfold!*—(from Vaughan) and *Let Much Be Enough!*"[6]—(based perhaps on Blake's "Enough! or Too much" from *The Marriage of Heaven and Hell*). Since there is no poem in the Roethke canon with the second title, he must have decided that "much" was already quite "enough."

Originally "I Cry, Love! Love!" (the poem following "Unfold! Unfold!") was the last poem of the *Praise to the End!* sequence; but when *The Waking*, Roethke's selected poems from 1933 to 1953, appeared, there was one more added to the end—"O, Thou Opening, O." The very fact that Roethke chose the titles for these two final pieces from love poems indicates the direction in which he was planning to move. He is still dealing with the relationship between self and other, as he is in his poems of childhood and nature, but now the "other" is specifically another human being. The first title mentioned is from Oothoon's lament at the end of Blake's *Visions of the Daughters of Albion*:

> I cry: Love! Love! Love! happy happy Love! free
> as the mountain wind!
> Can that be Love that drinks another as a sponge
> drinks water,
> That clouds with jealousy his nights, with
> weeping all the day,
> To spin a web of age around him, grey and hoary,
> dark,
> Till his eyes sicken at the fruit that hangs
> before his sight?
> Such is self-love that envies all . . .
> (Plate 7, lines 16-21)

Oothoon makes a distinction between "self love," which restricts one's vision and one's energy, and that "generous love" (line 29) that "brings expansion to the eye" (line 33). By freely loving others, Blake suggests, one can share their

[6] *Selected Letters*, p. 155.

lives and their visions and thus expand one's own experiences and vision. In "I Cry, Love! Love!" Roethke states his desire to join with another and thereby to increase the range of his poetry:

> A dry cry comes from my own desert;
> The bones are lonely. . . .
> We never enter
> Alone.
>
> (CP 93)

"Delight me otherly," he cries, playing on the word "utterly" while emphasizing his need for "the other." According to Blake, by loving, one expands one's visionary state: Roethke, by writing about love, can "break from self-involvement, from I to Otherwise"[7] and can expand the state of his poetry.

The title of the last poem in the sequence, "O, Thou Opening, O," again suggests an expansion into new experiences; and since the title echoes the line "Oh, open the door to me, oh!" from a love lyric by Robert Burns, we see once more that these experiences are to be achieved through love. Among the many new objects for Roethke's affection will be, of course, the poets of the past whom he will use in writing his new poetry. When he states in "O, Thou Opening, O" that "A son has many fathers," he makes it clear that he will not limit himself to those poets, particularly the Romantics Blake, Wordsworth, and Coleridge, whom he has already extensively explored in his two long sequences, but he will find the other "fathers" he needs, to invent his very own tradition.

Roethke's first step in opening himself up to new influences was the re-acceptance of traditional verse forms. In his earliest poetry he merely accepted standard verse patterns without questioning their implications for the modern poet. Through his second two volumes he avoided traditional patterns in an attempt to structure his poems

7 "On 'Identity,'" *On the Poet and His Craft*, p. 25.

through association of ideas and recurring images that develop into archetypal symbols. Now in the new poems (1951-1953) in *The Waking* he has returned to traditional forms and consciously uses them as both a means and a subject for his poetry—altering and reanimating the old forms through those various and energetic techniques he learned in his sequence poems.

In "The Waking" Roethke attempted to inject some vitality into that most structured of verse forms, the villanelle. He wished to use it not as a mode for light verse (as had the Victorians), but as a vehicle for serious themes. In effect, one of those serious themes is the form of the poem. When Roethke writes, "I learn by going where I have to go," he is making a statement not only about life but also about the very form of art he is using. There is indeed a direction in which a poet has to go when he writes a villanelle, but the conscious artist, rather than giving himself to the mechanics of the verse, can learn something of himself by following the form. After "the longish pieces that really break the ground—if any ground is broken,"[8] Roethke returns to writing poetry in which "the ground beat of the great tradition can be heard, with the necessary subtle variations."[9] Poetry is a combination of the individual creative choices of the artist and of the inherited traditions of linguistic and poetic forms; and, in that combination, all poetry implies in its structure the eternal argument between free will and fate, which is the explicit theme of "The Waking." Roethke has moved from being a poet who struggles with his inheritance to a poet who accepts the burden and finds his fate in what he no longer fears.

Throughout his poetry Roethke implicitly and explicitly acknowledges his Dancing Masters, those poets, past and present, who influenced his life and art. Nowhere in his work

[8] "Theodore Roethke Writes . . . ," *On the Poet and His Craft*, p. 60.

[9] Roethke uses this phrase to describe Louise Bogan's poetry in his essay, "The Poetry of Louise Bogan," *On the Poet and His Craft*, p. 148.

does this process reveal itself more clearly and take on more importance than in "Four for Sir John Davies," published in *The Waking* (1953), with its sections entitled "The Dance," "The Partner," "The Wraith," and "The Vigil." Although Roethke writes in "Four for Sir John Davies," "I take this cadence from a man named Yeats," in his essay "How to Write Like Somebody Else," he says that this line "is in a sense, a fib" and that Ralegh and Davies "rather than Willie are the true ghosts in that piece." He explains the "important technical difference" separating his style from Yeats's and linking it to the plain style of the sixteenth century: "in the pentameter, I end-stop almost every line—a thing more usual when the resources of the language were more limited. . . . It is part of an effort, however clumsy, to bring the language back to bare, hard, even terrible statement."[10] Nevertheless, within the line, Roethke consciously plays against the iambic pattern in the same way that Yeats does and manages to achieve that distinctively Yeatsian tone and rhythm, so difficult to describe but so easy to recognize, that we connect with the Byzantium poems and "Among School Children." The point is that Roethke brings together techniques from both Davies and Yeats to form that new compound, his poem. At the conclusion of "Orchestra or, a Poem on Dancing," the sixteenth-century work serving as one of the major sources for what Roethke called his "poems on 'dancing,' "[11] Davies also invokes both dead poets (Virgil, Chaucer, Sidney) and living ones (Spenser, Samuel Daniel, Richard Martin).[12] Just as Davies dedicates "Orchestra" to Richard Martin and wishes he could "borrow" Spenser's "fair heroic style" and "smooth" his "rhymes" as Daniel

[10] "How to Write Like Somebody Else," *On the Poet and His Craft*, p. 70.

[11] See *Selected Letters*, letter to Kenneth Burke, November 5, 1953, p. 181.

[12] Sir John Davies, "Orchestra," in *Silver Poets of the Sixteenth Century*, ed. Gerald Bullett (London: Dent, 1947), p. 341. All subsequent quotations from "Orchestra" are from this edition, which was the text owned and annotated by Roethke. The text is the same as E. M. W. Tillyard's edition of *Orchestra* (London, 1947).

does, Roethke dedicates his poem to Davies and desires to "take [his] cadence from a man named Yeats." Roethke, like Davies, explicitly refers to a tradition of poets to provide a context for the creation and appreciation of his own work. The theme of "Four for Sir John Davies" is the reconcilement of contraries; by borrowing from both Davies and Yeats, one conjunction Roethke effects is between the poets of the past and the poets of the present.

The conceptual contrasts in Roethke's poem are made definite in the vocabulary: "alone" and "commingled," "take . . . and . . . give," "teach" and "learn," "heart and . . . brain," "animal and human heat," "the body and the soul," "gaiety and dread," "behind, before," "the spirit and the flesh," "each" and "the other," "out and . . . in," "valley" and "hill," "dark and light," "was and was not," "black" and "white," "the dead" and "the living," "rise" and "fall." The implicit oppositions include male and female, form and chaos, life and art. Roethke turns to several poets for images to conciliate these contraries. From Davies he borrows the basic structural image for his poem—"the dance," itself a symbol of the harmonious union of order and energy, or, as Davies writes, "Dancing" is "the child of Music and of Love" (line 667). For the sixteenth-century poet, to participate in a dance on earth is to bring the self into tune with divine harmony, since all the ordered motions of the world reflect universal order. The first lines of Roethke's "The Dance" deal with the lesser harmony "in the mind of man" and the greater harmony of "the universe." The modern poet asks if there is still a relationship between them. He answers by suggesting that through the rhythms he creates in his own art he will try to take part in the rhythms of all creation:

> The great wheel turns its axle when it can;
> I need a place to sing, and dancing-room,
> And I have made a promise to my ears
> I'll sing and whistle romping with the bears.
> (CP 105)

Roethke is identifying himself not only "with the shambling but pleasurable gait of bears," as Ralph J. Mills, Jr. suggests,[13] but also with the systematic movement of the constellations *Ursa Major* and *Ursa Minor*, as can be seen by comparing Roethke's quatrain with the following lines from "Orchestra" describing God's transformation of chaos into order:

> As the two Bears, whom the First Mover flings
> With a short turn about heaven's axletree,
> In a round dance for ever wheeling be.
>
> (lines 446-448)

Roethke dances with the earthly bears in the rhythms of nature and with the celestial bears in the measured motions of the universe, just as he and Davies try to write poetry that follows the example of other earthly poets and that also echoes the music of the spheres. Davies tries to

> knock at heaven's great gate above
> With my proud rhymes, while of this heavenly state
> I do aspire the shadow to relate.
>
> (lines 915-917)

He sees his own verse as a reflection ("shadow") of the greater cosmic harmony. By "heaven's great gate," he means the moon, since it is the sphere of the moon that separates the world of mutability from the immortal world.[14] Following Davies (and not Yeats, as others have suggested),[15] Roethke writes, "I tried to fling my shadow at the moon." He also borrows Davies' idea that the dance "doth compound in one" the oppositions of man and woman. Davies writes, "For in this dance their arms they so imply/As each

13 Ralph J. Mills, Jr., *Theodore Roethke*, p. 32.

14 See, for example, Edmund Spenser, *Two Cantos of Mutabilities*, Canto VI, verse viii, where Spenser calls "the circle of the Moone" the "silver gates" between the world governed by "Tyme" and the immutable world of heaven.

15 See, for example, Malkoff, p. 117.

doth seem the other to enfold." Roethke asks the rhetorical question, "Did each become the other in that play?"

This line provides the reader with an opportunity to study on a small scale the way in which Roethke's powers of association function. Davies in his line just quoted was referring specifically to "Venus and Mars." These figures suggested to Roethke another Renaissance work about Mars and Venus, Shakespeare's *Antony and Cleopatra*.[16] The very first sentence of the play likens Antony to "plated Mars"[17] (see also II, ii, 6: II, v, 118), and Cleopatra in the famous passage describing her arrival on the barge (II, ii, 200) is compared to, and found to surpass, Venus. Compare Roethke's lines with Shakespeare's:

> Did each become the other in that play?
> She laughed me out, and then she laughed me in.
> ("The Wraith")

> Cleopatra:
> I laughed him out of patience; and that night
> I laughed him into patience . . .
> I put my tires and mantles on him, whilst
> I wore his sword Philippan.
> (II, v, 19-20, 22-23)

Antony and Cleopatra were literally "two, together, on a darkening day" (compare Shakespeare's "declining day" v, i, 38) who "took arms against [their] own obscurity." In a poem about the reconcilement of contraries, Roethke's implicit references to Shakespeare's Cleopatra, who describes herself as "fire and air" (v, ii, 288) and who has been de-

[16] Roethke must have known Shakespeare's play quite well. He wrote, in a letter from Bennington to Allan Seager on May 8, 1943, "I teach three courses 'Literature and Humanities' (a freshman course which emphasizes close reading of the text—various versions of *Antony & Cleopatra* . . .)," *Selected Letters*, p. 109.

[17] *Antony and Cleopatra*, The Arden Edition of the Works of William Shakespeare, ed. M. R. Ridley (New York: Random House, 1967), p. 3. All subsequent quotations from the play are from this edition.

scribed by various critics as "a brilliant antithesis," "a compound of contradictions," and a "glorious riddle, whose dazzling complexity continually mocks and eludes us,"[18] are most apt. Cleopatra must surely have been the model for Roethke's "partner"—"That woman" who "would set sodden straw on fire." It may seem as if I am giving disproportionate attention to some rather obvious references to *Antony and Cleopatra.* Let me use John Livingston Lowes's argument in a similar situation when "through the association of obviously linked ideas, a new combination was effected." "In itself," he writes, "it could scarcely be more trivial. As an index of processes through which new shapes of beauty may be created, its significance is not easy to exaggerate."[19]

Just as Roethke moves from Davies to Shakespeare because of a single mythological allusion to Venus and Mars common to both, he also moves from Davies to Yeats, the only other poet besides the author of "Orchestra" to make such extensive use of the image and thematic significance of the dance. The contraries in Yeats's "dance" are the artist and the artifact. Yeats uses the image of dancing as an expression of an activity in which the creator and the thing created are one: "O body swayed to music, O brightening glance,/How can we know the dancer from the dance?" ("Among School Children").[20] Yeats's answer is that we cannot know: the human form is not distinguishable from the ideal artistic form. Through Roethke's implicit references to "Among School Children" (his line "O watch his body sway" echoing Yeats's "O body swayed to music") and his explicit ones ("a man named Yeats," "Yeats would know"), Roethke makes it clear that he too strives for a fusion of the self (the artist) and the other (the art work). When Roethke writes, "I'd say it to my horse: we live

[18] See Ridley's introduction to the Arden Edition, p. xiv.

[19] John Livingston Lowes, *The Road to Xanadu* (Boston: Houghton Mifflin, 1927), p. 318.

[20] *The Collected Poems of W. B. Yeats* (New York: Macmillan, 1956), p. 214. All further quotations from Yeats are from this edition.

beyond/Our outer skin," he obliquely refers to another image from Yeats—the image of the horse and the rider that, like the dancer and the dance, is a concord of contraries. For Yeats the horseman represents the intellect, the horse represents passion, and together they symbolize the proper combination of order and energy that characterizes all of man's best works, including poetry (see especially "Coole Park and Ballylee, 1931").

By referring to Yeats's symbol for the productive harmony between passion and intellect, Roethke can next move on to a consideration of the conflict of "the body and the soul." To find a means for a resolution of the oppositions between the physical life and the spiritual life, he moves at the end of "The Wraith" towards images suggesting the figure of the idealized woman who contains in herself and harmonizes both flesh and spirit. Roethke asks, Are the contraries of body and soul really harmonized in the image of the ideal woman? His question is embodied in the poem in the dialectic between statements that on the one hand show how the flesh leads to the spirit ("The flesh can make the spirit visible") and on the other hand show how the flesh compromises and detracts from the spiritual ("The visible obscures"). He begins "The Vigil" with the name of that poet who epitomizes the tradition of the idealization of woman. Dante resolved the conflict between body and soul through the image of Beatrice, who begins in *La Vita Nuova* as a young girl and ends in the *Paradiso* as one of Dante's guides to a vision of God. Through intellectualizing his desire for this woman, he is led upward to a love of the spirit. Roethke questions the validity of the Dantean experience and looks skeptically at the whole process of idealizing a woman, especially as that process is embodied in Dante's poetry:

> Dante attained the purgatorial hill,
> Trembled at hidden virtue without flaw,
> Shook with a mighty power beyond his will,—

Did Beatrice deny what Dante saw?
All lovers live by longing, and endure:
Summon a vision and declare it pure.

Writing from the perspective of the Dantean vision of Beatrice and in terms of the whole course of Dante's journey in *The Divine Comedy* from the dark wood to the ultimate light, the speaker in the last stanza of "The Vigil" returns to his own experience with a woman. They participated in bodily existence, he explains, to reach the ecstatic experience of love that goes beyond the flesh and involves the spirit and the intellect. "We dared the dark to reach the white and warm," Roethke writes, showing a parallel between this experience with a woman and that great literary journey of Dante's in which he arrives at the pure white light by first going down into the darkness of Hell. When Roethke writes, "Who rise from flesh to spirit know the fall," he simultaneously states a literal fact about Dante's journey, shows the progression of the figure of Beatrice, and comments upon his love relationship with the woman in the poem. Roethke's final statement suggests that even if the Dantean experience is found only in poetry, the imaginative act of literary creation is itself a means by which we are lifted up from physical existence into a realization of spiritual life: "The word outleaps the world, and light is all." At the conclusion of "Four for Sir John Davies," as at the conclusion of the *Paradiso* (canto xxxiii), the image of the idealized woman ends and the image of pure spiritual light filling all space begins. There is a final absorption of all contraries into a single, completely whole, completely perfect being—God as imaged as light.

The end of Pope's *Dunciad* is a parody of the creation; the end of Roethke's poem is a further serious parodying of Pope. Hence, by reversing Pope and at the same time using his vocabulary, Roethke brings us back to creative rather than destructive energies. Book IV of the *Dunciad* ends

Nor public Flame, nor private, dares to shine;
Nor human Spark is left, nor Glimpse divine!
Lo! thy dread Empire, Chaos! is restored;
Light dies before thy uncreating word:
Thy hand, great Anarch! lets the curtain fall;
And universal Darkness buries All.
(lines 651-656)[21]

Roethke writes in "The Vigil," "We undid chaos" and "We danced to shining" and then concludes

The world is for the living. Who are they?
We dared the dark to reach the white and warm.
She was the wind when wind was in my way;
Alive at noon, I perished in her form.
Who rise from flesh to spirit know the fall:
The word outleaps the world, and light is all.

Roethke's entire poem is finally an extended conceit in which the poet simultaneously makes statements about actual experiences and constructs and comments upon his literary tradition, specifically that tradition of poetry in which contraries are harmonized. "The lively dead"—Dante, Davies, Shakespeare, Pope, and Yeats—are assimilated into a structure at once both a poem and a concept of tradition.

In his essay "On 'Identity,' " Roethke describes the intense emotional experience of writing "Four for Sir John Davies":

"I was in that particular hell of the poet: a longish dry period. It was 1952, I was 44, and I thought I was done. I was living alone in a biggish house in Edmonds, Washington. I had been reading—and re-reading—not Yeats, but Ralegh and Sir John Davies. I had been teaching the five-beat line for weeks—I knew quite a bit about it, but write it myself? —*no*: so I felt myself a fraud.

"Suddenly, in the early evening, the poem 'The Dance'

[21] Alexander Pope, *The Dunciad*, ed. James Sutherland (New Haven: Yale University Press, 1963), p. 409.

started, and finished itself in a very short time—say thirty minutes, maybe in the greater part of an hour, it was all done. I felt, I *knew*, I had hit it. I walked around, and I wept; and I knelt down—I always do after I've written what I know is a good piece. But at the same time I had, as God is my witness, the actual sense of a Presence—as if Yeats himself were *in* that room. The experience was in a way terrifying, for it lasted at least half an hour. That house, I repeat, was charged with a psychic presence: the very walls seemed to shimmer. I wept for joy. At last I was somebody again. He, they—the poets dead—were with me."[22]

Roethke's conscious discovery and creation of a tradition pale beside this visionary experience in which he sensed direct contact with his literary ancestors. No more clear evidence could be presented for Roethke's deep and abiding faith in the crucial importance of tradition for his individual talent.

Roethke's way of creating was not mere imitation. It was an attempt to connect with another sensibility, to merge, finally to "see and suffer [himself] in another being, at last" (CP 126). For Roethke, writing poetry was like making love: it was an activity requiring a partner. All of his poems are literary love-children, the issue of a union between Roethke's own vision and the work of other poets whom he admired. Love became for Roethke one of his structural metaphors for this relationship between himself and his poetic partners, and in turn the writing of poetry became a metaphor for the act of love.

In his major sequence of Love Poems, which appeared in *Words for the Wind*, 1958, Roethke's response to the woman he loves is simultaneously a response to the poets he loves. The presence of his naked lover transforms Roethke into that very poet whose sensibility suggests the proper response to the woman: "I am my father's son, I am John Donne/ Whenever I see her with nothing on" ("The Swan," CP

[22] "On 'Identity,'" pp. 23-24.

140). Donne exhorts in one of his poems, "Study me then, you who shall lovers bee at the next world." Few of his followers have studied him as intently as Roethke, who learned from Donne a pattern for his love. Roethke's lines, however, leave the causal relationships between lover and poet ambiguous. Does the naked lover call forth emotions in Roethke's mind that he then associates with Donne, or does Donne's poetry conjure up the image of the woman? These images in "The Swan" embody that always complex relationship between the poet's personal experiences and his literary influences.

In the first poem of his sequence Roethke adopts both the title and the theory of one of Donne's love elegies. Louis L. Martz, in *The Meditative Poem*, suggests that Donne's "Elegy X," usually called "The Dreame," may "owe something to St. Augustine's theory that the soul always knows the 'image' of its beloved before meeting the beloved object."[23] Roethke's "The Dream" begins, "I met her as a blossom on a stem/Before she ever breathed" (CP 119). With the movement from the mind, to sight, to an image of fire, the next few lines of Roethke's poem recall William Drummond of Hawthornden's sequence of similar images—also to describe the speaker's foreknowledge of the beloved:

> My Minde mee told that in some other Place
> It elsewhere saw the Idea of that Face,
> And lov'd a Love of heavenly pure Delight.
> No Wonder now I feele so faire a Flame,
> Sith I Her lov'd ere on this Earth shee came.
> (Drummond)[24]

[23] See Commentary to *The Meditative Poem: An Anthology of Seventeenth-Century Verse*, ed. Louis L. Martz (New York: Doubleday and Company, 1963), p. 532. In *The Poems of John Donne*, ed. Sir Herbert Grierson (London: Oxford University Press, 1929), "Elegy X" is entitled "The Dreame."

[24] From Sonnet VII. Roethke must have been quite familiar with Drummond's poetry because he assigned the line "I long to kisse the Image of my Death" from Drummond's Sonnet IX ("Sleepe, Silence Child") to his students in his verse writing classes as a first line with which to start their own poems.

The mind remembers from a deeper sleep:
Eye learned from eye, cold lip from sensual lip.
My dream divided on a point of fire.
(Roethke)

Roethke, like Drummond, moves from self (mind) to other (fire), from inner to outer, through the organ of perception. The eye is also the portal through which love first enters man's soul in the traditions of Neo-Platonic and courtly love. The borrowings in any one of Roethke's love poems are seldom limited to a single poet: the doctrine of "The Dream" is from Donne and Drummond, the diction and the rhythm of some of the lines come from another Renaissance writer of love poetry—Sir Walter Ralegh. Compare, for example, Roethke's "She loved the wind because the wind loved me" with Ralegh's "I loved myself because myself loved you."

The celebration of the love relationship is in many of the poems in Roethke's sequence a kind of religious experience. In several poems, such as "The Dream," he, with his method of describing a sexual relationship as a spiritual experience expressed through traditional literary images, is very close to D. H. Lawrence, another twentieth-century writer who treats love as a central religious experience. Compare the following passage from Lawrence's novel *The Rainbow* with the end of Roethke's "The Dream":

"Inside the room was a great steadiness, a core of living eternity. Only far outside, at the rim, went on the noise and the destruction. Here at the centre the great wheel was motionless, centered upon itself. Here was a poised, unflawed stillness that was beyond time, because it remained the same, inexhaustible, unchanging, unexhausted. . . . The flames swept over him, he held her in sinews of fire. . . . He stood near the door in blackness of shadow, watching, transfixed. And with slow, heavy movements she swayed backwards and forwards." (*The Rainbow*, chapter vi.)[25]

[25] D. H. Lawrence, *The Rainbow* (New York: Viking, 1961), pp. 141, 152, 180. This novel was first published in 1915. Except for *Love*

She held her body steady in the wind;
Our shadows met, and slowly swung around;
She turned the field into a glittering sea;
I played in flame and water like a boy
And I swayed out beyond the white seafoam;
Like a wet log, I sang within a flame.
In that last while, eternity's confine,
I came to love, I came into my own.

(CP 120)

Through words and expressions such as "point," "encircled," "the center," "circles," and "least motion," Roethke images the love experience in terms similar to Lawrence's. The two poets, by describing love through the spatial metaphors of the circle and the point in the center of the circle, image secular love through Dante's metaphors for holy love in the *Paradiso*. Similarly, the states of "eternity" and "steadiness," in which the lover and his beloved reside, and the references to "fire" take on religious connotations. Roethke, following Lawrence and the seventeenth-century metaphysical poets, carries the love relationship between man and woman to a higher level of spiritual insight by means of images and metaphors traditionally reserved for religious subjects. In "The Dream" Roethke writes of love primarily by joining in a poetically intimate relationship with other talents.

Lawrence's love poems, as well as his novels, furnish Roethke with points of departure for his own love lyrics. "I Wish I Knew a Woman" expresses Lawrence's desire for an ideal sexual relationship: Roethke's "I Knew a Woman" presents such a relationship in its consummation. Roethke not only draws upon the poets in his tradition for images and themes, he also continually struggles to outdo these other poets. His well-known love poem begins,

---

Poems and Others, The Rainbow is the only work of Lawrence's on the list of "Annotated Volumes in the Theodore Roethke Collection," University of Washington.

I knew a woman, lovely in her bones,
When small birds sighed, she would sigh back
  at them;
Ah, when she moved, she moved more ways than
  one:
The shapes a bright container can contain!
Of her choice virtues only gods should speak,
Or English poets who grew up on Greek
(I'd have them sing in chorus, cheek to cheek).

How well her wishes went! She stroked my chin,
She taught me Turn, and Counter-turn, and Stand;
She taught me Touch, that undulant white skin;
I nibbled meekly from her proffered hand;
She was the sickle; I, poor I, the rake,
Coming behind her for her pretty sake
(But what prodigious mowing we did make).

(CP 127)

Since "English poets who grew up on Greek" are best able to sing this woman's praises, it is to these poets that Roethke turns for metaphors and images. One poet who fits the description and whom we are inevitably reminded of when we read Roethke's extended metaphor on "mowing" is Andrew Marvell. Although the "mowing" image is predominant in several of Marvell's poems ("The Mower against Gardens," "Damon the Mower," and "The Mower to the Glo-Worms"), it is in the refrain to "The Mower's Song" that the description of scything is most clearly a metaphor for the sexual relationship with a woman: "When Julianna came, and She/What I do to the Grass, does to my Thoughts and Me." Roethke, like Marvell, brings new life to the convention-ridden pastoral love lyric through the injection into his poem of the intellectualized sensuality of metaphysical wit.

Roethke refers to another English poet who grew up on Greek when he writes, "She taught me Turn, and Counter-turn, and Stand." The source for this unusual way of naming the three divisions of an ode (commonly called "strophe," "antistrophe," and "epode") is probably Ben Jonson's "To the Immortal Memorie, and Friendship of that Noble Paire, Sir Lucius Cary, and Sir H. Morison," in which the terms "the Turne," "the Counter-Turne," and "the Stand" are used as titles for the various sections of the poem. The verbal echo in and of itself is slight, but it is only through a knowledge of this echo that we realize an important theme in Roethke's poem. By employing these literary terms in his line, Roethke describes the rhythm of love as a movement in poetry. He not only transforms life into art, he also perceives and thus images it as art. This metaphor, imaging sex as poetry, has its converse in a mocking title scribbled in one of Roethke's notebooks: "Thirteen Ways of Fornicating the Amphibrach." In an even more general formulation of the union of poetry and sex, sex and poetry, Roethke wrote down a few pages later in this same notebook a line from Becquer: "Poetry is feeling and feeling is woman."[26]

One of the most remarkable examples of Roethke's imagination coming to bear upon a text and transforming it into poetry is his use of St. Augustine's analysis of time in terms of bodily motion in the chapter on time and eternity in his *Confessions*: "When a body is moved, I measure in time how long it is moved."[27] Roethke's "I Knew a Woman" ends "But who would count eternity in days?/These old bones live to learn her wanton ways:/(I measure time by how a body sways)." Roethke takes "body" not just to mean a physical object, but to refer to the woman's body. In I. A. Richards' terms, he transforms the referential language of the philosopher and theologian into the emotive language

[26] Theodore Roethke Collection, University of Washington, Seattle (Notebooks, Box 44, #218 [1958]).

[27] *The Confessions of St. Augustine*, trans. John K. Ryan (New York, 1960), p. 296. The translation of this line is basically the same in all editions that I have checked, including F. J. Sheed's (New York, 1943), Edward B. Pusey's (New York, 1949), and William Watts's translation of 1631, reprinted in the Loeb Classical Library (Cambridge, Massachusetts, 1912).

of his poem. This converting of a sentence from Augustine at his most scientific into an image for a love poem shows the energy of Roethke's mind: he absorbed everything he read and with a few turns and counter-turns transmuted it into poetry. One cannot help being reminded of Pablo Picasso's "Bull's Head," which is made out of nothing more than the seat and handlebars of an old bicycle. The great attraction of the piece is the viewer's realization of the shaping vision of the artist, rather than the actual materials before him. "What is far from simple," writes H. W. Janson in the *History of Art*, "is the leap of the imagination by which Picasso recognized a bull's head in these unlikely objects. . . . Clearly, then, we must be careful not to confuse the making of a work of art with manual skill or craftsmanship."[28] Similarly, what we marvel at in Roethke's lines (so close to Augustine's) is not so much his technical skills as the genius and wit of his creative powers.

Although the immediate source for Roethke's image may be Augustine, the master of the method he uses to handle this image is Donne. Roethke, like Donne, takes sensual experiences and deals with them through scientific and theological imagery. He is thoroughly eclectic in searching out and in inventing specific images to describe the love experience, but his methodology is consistently in the tradition of Donne—that line of wit in love poetry that extends from the master of seventeenth-century metaphysical poetry through Lawrence and up to Roethke. This is indeed "Love's Progress"—as Roethke was well aware when he borrowed this title from Donne for one of his own poems—and simultaneously it is the progress of poetry.

The underlying pattern in metaphysical love poetry is the continual interplay between the mind and the body, between the thoughts of an inherently philosophical speaker and his emotions that form the heart of the love experience. The metaphysical poem moves out of this dramatic conflict and

[28] H. W. Janson, *History of Art* (Englewood Cliffs, N.J.: Prentice-Hall, n.d.), p. 10.

into its own drama of images, most characteristically in the extended conceit, where the elements of mind and body are fused. Roethke saw this same basic drama enacted in Yeats's poetry. Although we do not usually think of Yeats as essentially in the Donne tradition of love poetry, Roethke responds to him in a way that does point out the sympathies between the love poems of Yeats and the tradition of Donne. Compare the first stanza of Roethke's "The Pure Fury" with two passages from Yeats:

> Stupor of knowledge lacking inwardness—
> What book, O learned man, will set me right?
> Once I read nothing through a fearful night,
> For every meaning had grown meaningless.
> Morning, I saw the world with second sight,
> As if all things had died, and rose again.
> I touched the stones, and they had my own skin.
>
> ("The Pure Fury," CP 133)

> it sails into the sight
> And in the morning's gone, no man knows why;
> And is so lovely that it sets to right
> What knowledge or its lack had set awry,
> So arrogantly pure. . . .
>
> ("Coole Park and Ballylee, 1931")

> That every morning rose again. . . .
> For what mere book can grant a knowledge. . . .
> And must no beautiful woman be
> Learned like a man? . . . .
> That all must come to sight and touch. . . .
>
> ("Michael Robartes and the Dancer")

Both of Yeats's poems are about the powers of the body (and thus the powers of women) being radically different from and perhaps even superior to powers of masculine intellect. Loving a woman therefore can be quite a dangerous venture as these two beings—the woman-body and the man-mind—come together. This same drama is basic to

Roethke's poem, both in the speaker's attitude towards the woman and in the very images used to describe this attitude. Even though his poem is titled "The Pure Fury," it is still about Yeats's "complexities of fury" or "furies of complexity"—those intricate interrelationships between the physical and the spiritual. However, in calling it a "pure" fury, Roethke is perhaps trying to bring the metaphysical image to that ultimate plenum where mind and body become one. What Yeats does in his poems and what Roethke does also is not only to use the method of metaphysical love poetry but also to make this method a metaphor for love and finally the very subject of the poem.

By bringing Yeats into association with Donne, Drummond, Jonson, Marvell, and Lawrence, Roethke functions as both critic and poet: he offers us a new perspective on a major tradition in English love poetry. Many voices echo and breathe in unison through Roethke's love poems, and the harmonies that result reveal the underlying similarities between these diverse poets brought together by Roethke in a continuation of metaphysical wit to "sing [like lovers] in chorus, cheek to cheek."

From the poems of self and nature, Roethke has moved to a poetry in which the central relationship is between the poet and a lover. Frequently this "lover" is a woman explicitly imaged in the poem. But even in these love poems, the significant creative "lover" is the poet (or poets) with whom Roethke has joined. To love another (poet or woman) is finally to desire to merge with that person, and this can be accomplished linguistically by speaking as if one were the other. Thus Roethke's next sequence is an extended dramatic monologue.

VI

Meditations

As we have seen, Roethke is finally most original when he is most imitative, almost always returning to another poet as much as he has received from him. What is often difficult to determine exactly, however, is from which poet or what poem Roethke is borrowing. This has been a question critics have tried to answer about one of his finest sequences of long poems, *Meditations of an Old Woman*, in which an aging yet intellectually vital old crone prepares for death by trying to understand life. According to Roethke, the old woman is modeled, in part, after his own mother, "whose favorite reading was the Bible, Jane Austen, and Dostoevski—in other words, a gentle, highly articulate old lady believing in the glories of the world, yet fully conscious of its evils."[1] Roethke makes this person sound more like a combination of his own literary interests and Wallace Stevens' "A High-Toned Old Christian Woman" than like his mother Helen Roethke, who had little formal education and spent most of her life ironing, baking, cleaning, and washing. But then, "Poetry is the supreme fiction, madame." And, in this case, placing his mother within such a literary setting may be for Roethke a continuation of the process of creating his own tradition.

Several critics, including John Wain, W. D. Snodgrass, and Denis Donoghue, suggest that the form of these dramatic monologues is influenced by the Eliot of *Four Quartets*.[2] It is certainly true that there are significant similarities

[1] "Theodore Roethke Writes . . . ," *On the Poet and His Craft*, p. 58.

[2] See John Wain, "The Monocle of My Sea-Faced Uncle," p. 67, W. D. Snodgrass, " 'That Anguish of Concreteness'—Theodore Roethke's Career," p. 82, and Denis Donoghue, "Roethke's Broken Music," p. 160, all in *Theodore Roethke: Essays on the Poetry*.

between Eliot's and Roethke's sequences, but the reason for the resemblances is that they have a common source—Walt Whitman. Roethke's poetry demonstrates the living power of Whitman's voice among modern poets. "My point is this," wrote Roethke in a letter of 1959 to Ralph J. Mills, Jr. (whom Roethke, never able for an instant to cease being literary, called "Ralph Roister-Doister"), "I came to some of Eliot's and Yeats's ancestors long before I came to them; in fact, for a long time, I rejected both of them. . . . So what in the looser line may seem in the first old lady poem ['First Meditation'] to be close to Eliot may actually be out of Whitman, who influenced Eliot *plenty* [Roethke's emphasis], technically . . . —and Eliot, as far as I know, has never acknowledged this—oh no, he's always chi-chi as hell: only Dante, the French, the Jacobeans, etc."[3] Roethke then refers Mills to a study he has recently read, S. Musgrove's *T. S. Eliot and Walt Whitman*, "again not the whole truth, but a sensible book."[4] Musgrove's work, published in 1952, just before Roethke began writing his "Old Lady pieces" as he called them,[5] played an important role in Roethke's use of Whitman's and Eliot's techniques. The critic shows the striking similarities between the two poets and thereby provides Roethke with the protostructure of a tradition to draw upon for his poetry written in response to that tradition. Indeed, in his notebooks of this period Roethke quotes at some length from Musgrove's book, both Musgrove's critical statements and passages from Whitman and Eliot that the critic sets up for comparison.[6]

By borrowing Musgrove's points of comparison and his examples of Whitman's and Eliot's basic syntax[7] and adding

[3] *Selected Letters*, p. 230.

[4] *Selected Letters*, p. 230. [5] *Selected Letters*, p. 206.

[6] See especially Notebook #202 in Box 43. Theodore Roethke Collection, University of Washington, Seattle.

[7] S. Musgrove, *T. S. Eliot and Walt Whitman* (Wellington, New Zealand: University Press, 1952). Unless otherwise noted, all the following quotations from Musgrove are from pp. 24-28. All quotations from Eliot and Whitman are taken from Musgrove, but all passages so quoted have been checked against T. S. Eliot, *Collected*

to them examples from Roethke's *Meditations*, I intend to show the resemblances in the rhythms of the three poets. What follows may seem mechanical, but it is the best way to reconstruct Roethke's actual creative processes as he too compared Whitman, Eliot, and himself. Musgrove's role in suggesting these comparisons is central and reveals Roethke's self-creative use of a literary critic in a way that shows our profession in a remarkably favorable light.

All three poets place related clauses in a series without connecting words, but with repeated initial participles "acting as the recurrent link":

> Throwing myself on the sand, confronting the
> waves, . . .
> Taking all hints to use them, but swiftly
> leaping beyond them . . .
> (Whitman, "Out of the Cradle
> Endlessly Rocking")

> Worshipping snakes or trees, worshipping devils
> rather than nothing; crying for life beyond
> life, for ecstasy not of the flesh.
> (Eliot, "The Rock")

> Running through high grasses,
> My thighs brushing against flower-crowns;
> Leaning, out of all breath,
> Bracing my back against a sapling,
> Making it quiver with my body.
> (Roethke, "I'm Here," CP 161)

Poems 1909-1962 and Walt Whitman, *Leaves of Grass*, ed. Harold W. Blodgett and Sculley Bradley (New York: Norton, 1965). Musgrove explains that "stylistic parallels" of the kind that he points out "prove no more than a general 'current' of poetical development running from Whitman to Eliot" (pp. 30-31). But the discovery of just such a "current" was exactly what interested Roethke as the first step in the creation of his literary tradition. Musgrove, of course, deals with more than just general similarities in style.

Often the three poets use "a repeated preposition as the linking word":

> In the cars of railroads, in steamboats, in the
>   public assembly.
> ("Song of the Open Road")

> In the snow, in the rain, in the wind, in the
>   storm;
> in all of Thy creatures, both the hunters and
>   the hunted.
> (*Murder in the Cathedral*)

> In the sun, busy at a young body,
> In the rain, slackening on a summer field;
> In the back of my mind, running with the rolling
>   water.
> ("Her Becoming," CP 165)

Or a sequence of infinitives:

> To get the final lilt of songs,
> To penetrate the inmost lore of poets—to know
>   the mighty ones, . . .
> To diagnose the shifting-delicate tints of love
>   and pride and doubt—to truly understand,
> To encompass these . . .
> ("To Get the Final Lilt of Songs")

> To communicate with Mars, converse with spirits,
> To report the behaviour of the sea monster,
> Describe the horoscope, . . .
> To explore the womb, or tomb, or dreams.
> ("The Dry Salvages")

> What is it to be a woman?
> To be contained, to be a vessel?
> To prefer a window to a door? . . .

> To become lost in a love, . . .
> To be a mouth, a meal of meat?
> To gaze at a face with the fixed eyes of a
> spaniel?
> ("Fourth Meditation," CP 169)

"An interesting variant on the use of the repeated initial participle as a connecting link," writes Musgrove, "is the use of a series of terminal participles." The three poets employ these ending participles "in groups of lines which tend to stand out from the body of the poem as self contained paragraphs":

> Here and there with dimes on the eyes walking,
> To feed the greed of the belly the brains
> liberally spooning,
> Tickets buying, taking, selling, but in to the
> feast never once going,
> Many sweating, ploughing, thrashing, and then
> the chaff for payment receiving,
> A few idly owning, and they the wheat continually
> claiming.
> ("Song of Myself," stanza 42)

> Here are the years that walk between, bearing
> Away the fiddles and flutes, restoring
> One who moves in the time between sleep and
> waking, wearing . . .
> ("Ash-Wednesday," IV)

> So much of adolescence is an ill-defined dying,
> An intolerable waiting,
> A longing for another place and time,
> Another condition.
> ("I'm Here," CP 162)

The "final rhythmical resemblance" that Musgrove points out is an important one and holds as true for the Roethke of the *Meditations* as for Whitman and Eliot: ". . . each poet works in terms of the self-contained single line."

Roethke stated in "How to Write Like Somebody Else" that in the pentameter, he end-stopped almost every line.[8] In his long, looser lines he continues to avoid enjambement and, following Eliot following Whitman, to employ terminal pauses.

In addition to the "rhythmical resemblances," there are stylistic similarities among the poets. According to Musgrove, the most obvious point of resemblance between Whitman and Eliot is "the device sometimes called the 'catalogue': the list of instances, one crowding thickly after another, to illustrate and particularize the idea which lies at the center of the poem." Whitman's addiction to this device needs no substantiation. Eliot and Roethke acquired the habit from Whitman and use it often as an organizing device in their poetry. "There are areas of experience in modern life that simply cannot be rendered by either the formal lyric or straight prose," Roethke wrote. "We need the catalogue in our time."[9] In his last volume he invokes Whitman as the teacher of this technique: "Be with me, Whitman, maker of catalogues" ("The Abyss," CP 220). Musgrove demonstrates that "certain patterns of word order, which derive from this habit of cataloguing, are common to Eliot and Whitman. Both poets, for instance, gain emphasis . . . by powerful repetition of initial words, or repeated use of parallel clauses." Roethke shares with the two poets not only this technique of repeating the initial word but also "another verbal habit . . . connected with the habit of cataloguing—the obtrusiveness of the definite article." Part 3 of Whitman's "Song of the Broad-Axe" begins,

> The log at the wood-pile, the axe supported by it,
> The sylvan hut, the vine over the doorway, the
> space clear'd for a garden,
> The irregular tapping of rain down on the leaves
> after the storm is lull'd, . . .

[8] *On the Poet and His Craft*, p. 70.
[9] "Some Remarks on Rhythm," *On the Poet and His Craft*, p. 83.

and continues up to Part 4 with fifty-nine more lines beginning with "the." Although the poetry of Eliot and Roethke does not abound with quite so many articles, it echoes the parallelistic "the's" of Whitman (and ultimately of the King James Bible):

> The common word exact without vulgarity,
> The formal word precise but not pedantic,
> The complete consort dancing together . . .
> ("Little Gidding," v)

> The dance of natural objects in the mind,
> The immediate sheen, the reality of straw,
> The shadows crawling down a sunny wall.
> ("What Can I Tell My Bones?" CP 171)

Roethke has shifted to the indefinite article and away from the demonstrative pronoun of his Yeatsian poems, such as "Four for Sir John Davies" ("Is that dance slowing in the mind of man." "That woman would set sodden straw on fire").

One device not mentioned by Musgrove, since it is not found in Eliot's poetry, is the structuring of a poem or long passage around a single, isolated image. James E. Miller, Jr., in *A Critical Guide to Leaves of Grass*, explains that "the same genius that enabled Whitman to assemble the items of a catalogue and discover in the total a significance greater than the sum of all the parts endowed him also with keen poetic insight into the brief vignettes life seems always freely presenting to the perception."[10] One of the poems that illustrates this "technique of the 'caught' picture" is "A Noiseless Patient Spider," which has as its central device "the single image vividly dramatized":

> A noiseless patient spider,
> I mark'd where on a little promontory it stood
> isolated,

[10] James E. Miller, Jr., *A Critical Guide to Leaves of Grass* (Chicago: University of Chicago Press, 1957), p. 150.

Mark'd how to explore the vacant vast surrounding,
It launch'd forth filament, filament, filament,
out of itself,
Ever unreeling them, ever tirelessly speeding
them.

Then, "instead of letting the description stand by itself," Miller writes, "Whitman makes direct symbolic application":[11]

And you O my soul where you stand,
Surrounded, detached, in measureless oceans of
space,
Ceaselessly musing, venturing, throwing, seeking
the spheres to connect them,
Till the bridge you will need be form'd, till
the ductile anchor hold,
Till the gossamer thread you fling catch somewhere,
O my soul.

In his essay "Some Remarks on Rhythm," Roethke, after stressing the need for the catalogue in our time, states that also "we need the eye close on the object, and the poem about the single incident. . . . We must realize, I think, that the writer in freer forms must have an even greater fidelity to his subject matter than the poet who has the support of form."[12] Roethke, like Whitman, constructs poems and parts of poems on the single image. Compare his noiseless, patient crab to Whitman's spider:

As when silt drifts and sifts down through muddy
pond-water,
Settling in small beads around weeds and sunken
branches,
And one crab, tentative, hunches himself before
moving along the bottom,

[11] James E. Miller, Jr., p. 154.
[12] "Some Remarks on Rhythm," p. 83.

Grotesque, awkward, his extended eyes looking
 at nothing in particular,
Only a few bubbles loosening from the ill-matched
 tentacles,
The tail and smaller legs slipping and sliding
 slowly backward—

Roethke, too, brings the activities of his arthropod into relation with himself:

So the spirit tries for another life,
Another way and place in which to continue.
("First Meditation," part 3, CP 159)

"The eye close on the object" is justifiably the basic perspective in all the *Meditations of an Old Woman* since meditation itself, as Louis L. Martz explains, is that "discipline directed toward creating the 'act of pure attention' which D. H. Lawrence saw as essential to all significant discovery or decision: 'you choose that object to concentrate upon which will best focus your consciousness.' "[13]

According to Musgrove, Whitman and Eliot "isolate the image to the point where it becomes a consciously constructed and deliberately maintained symbol," and they repeat from one poem to another their "more important images as permanent recurring symbols."[14] This mode, common to all symbolist poets, of creating a symbol through the repetition of a single image, is also found in much of Roethke's poetry; it would be most informative to trace one of these images, such as "the bird," through all of his work —from "No Bird" in his first volume through "a delirium of birds" and finally in the last poem of his last volume to

[13] Louis L. Martz, "The Method of Meditation," *The Poetry of Meditation: A Study in English Religious Literature* (New Haven: Yale University Press, revised edition, 1962), p. 67. Martz's quotation from D. H. Lawrence appears in *Etruscan Places* (London: Martin Secker, 1932), pp. 97-99.

[14] Musgrove, p. 31.

"the Bird." "The hidden bird," Musgrove points out, is one of Whitman's recurring symbols and is "of all his symbols the one used most persistently by Eliot."[15] The figure of "the hidden bird" is also the central image in Roethke's *Meditations*, the old woman herself being the secluded bird. "I've become . . . bird-furtive," she says ("First Meditation"), and in "Her Becoming" she refers to herself as "A mad hen in a far corner of the dark." Finally, like the protagonist in "Out of the Cradle Endlessly Rocking," who identifies with the "singer solitary," she identifies with the "bird," who "sings out in solitariness/A thin harsh song" ("What Can I Tell My Bones?"). This image of the hidden bird clearly linking together Whitman and Eliot allows Roethke to see these poets as part of one tradition and allows the reader to ascribe many of the details in the *Meditations* to Roethke's combined memory of them. His uses of tradition have developed a long way from his early obvious borrowings from single poets. In this sequence he meditates upon and makes use of a double strain, both the parent (Eliot) and the ancestor (Whitman).

"I took your advice about making my old lady less lit'ry," Roethke wrote to William Carlos Williams in 1958;[16] but she remains a truly "literary" personality since she is modeled in response to characters in poetry. The "old woman" listening to "the weeds hiss at the edge of the field" in the opening stanzas of "First Meditation" is based upon the persona of Eliot's "old man" hearing "the goats cough at night in the field" in "Gerontion" and upon the figure in "A Song for Simeon" who "has eighty years and no tomorrow." Simeon is old and tired, waiting for death.

> My life is light, waiting for the death wind, . . .
> Wait for the wind that chills toward the
> dead land.
>
> (lines 4, 7)

[15] Musgrove, p. 67.

[16] *Selected Letters*, p. 221.

Roethke's old woman also lives in a dead land where "a tree tilts from its roots" and where

> The small winds make their chilly indictments. . . .
> What's left is light as a seed.
> ("First Meditation," part 1)

Roethke has consciously imitated the tone and the point of view, as well as the vocabulary, of Eliot, and for a reason—to reveal the fundamental contrast between his old woman and Eliot's old men and further to show that he can take "this Whitmanesque meditative thing," as he calls it, and "use it as well or better" than Eliot. He wrote to Ralph J. Mills, Jr.,

"As for the old lady poems, I wanted (1) to create a character for whom such rhythms [Whitman's] are indigenous; that she be a dramatic character, not just me. Christ, Eliot in the Quartets is tired, spiritually tired, old-man. Rhythm, Tiresome Tom. Is my old lady tired? The hell she is: she's tough, she's brave, she's aware of life and she would take a congeries of eels over a hassle of bishops any day. (2) Not only is Eliot tired, he's a [. . .] fraud as a mystic—all his moments in the rose-garden and the wind up his ass in the draughty-smoke-fall-church yard.

"Ach, how vulgar I become—perhaps."[17]

Fascinatingly and characteristically, Roethke, in the very act of reviling "Tiresome Tom, the Cautious Cardinal,"[18] reveals his close knowledge of Eliot's poetry.

Apparently, Roethke's vision of Whitman had been strongly affected, and in some ways distorted, by Eliot's use of Whitman. Therefore, to regain direct contact with Whitman, Roethke had to understand, practice, and then reject the "Whitmanesque meditative thing of T. S. E." His movement from Eliot to Whitman is clearly shown in the following lines:

[17] *Selected Letters*, p. 231. [18] *Selected Letters*, p. 154.

What's left is light as a seed;
I need an old crone's knowing.
("First Meditation," part 1)

As pointed out above, the first of these two lines echoes Eliot, but the second line refers to Whitman's "old crone rocking the cradle" in "Out of the Cradle Endlessly Rocking." Eliot's old men are aged in both body and spirit, but Roethke's old woman and Whitman's crone, like Yeats's Crazy Jane, who is "tired of cursing the Bishop" and would doubtless prefer the eels, know the vital center of life's energies. Finally Roethke's old lady becomes much like Whitman himself in *Sands at Seventy*, both, of course, in the patterns of her speech and in her ability to seize life even though it's about gone. She matches many of Whitman's descriptions of himself, such as,

Soon to be lost for aye in the darkness—loth,
O so loth to depart!
Garrulous to the very last.
("After the Supper and Talk")

The *Meditations* are the old woman's song of herself: just as Whitman asks and then investigates in "Song of Myself" "What is a man anyhow? What am I?" (section 20), she questions "What is it to be a woman?" ("Fourth Meditation"). In many sections of Roethke's sequence the speaker goes "backward in time" to memories of her girlhood. The first of these remembered experiences is based on the child's "reminiscence" in "Out of the Cradle Endlessly Rocking." The basic structure of both works is intrinsically the same—the adult mind recreates a childhood experience. The adult in Whitman's poem remembers when, as a boy, he saw a pair of mocking birds, "Two feather'd guests . . ." and heard "out of the mockingbird's throat, the musical shuttle." The old woman in "First Meditation" is also transported back to her youth to a memory of "two song sparrows, one within a greenhouse,/Shuttling its throat." The bird from Whitman in the greenhouse of Roethke's childhood shows metaphorically that the literary tradition is contained within the private memory.

In the second poem in the sequence of *Meditations*, Roethke, for both his title and his concluding lines, is again indebted to Whitman:

> Here I am! here! . . .
> That is the whistle of the wind . . .
> ("Out of the Cradle . . . ," 112 & 116)

> If the wind means me,
> I'm here!
> Here.
> ("I'm Here," part 5)

Since the second meditation is composed mainly of memories from the old woman's childhood, it is apt that "Out of the Cradle Endlessly Rocking" (first published under the title "A Child's Reminiscence") should be a source.

"All journeys," muses the old woman, "are the same: /The movement is forward, after a few wavers" and then there is a movement "backward,/Backward in time" ("First Meditation"). These lines describe exactly Roethke's method in both the *Meditations* and in his earlier sequences. As he wrote about *The Lost Son* poems, "I believe that to go forward . . . it is necessary first to go back. Any history of the psyche (or allegorical journey) is bound to be a succession of experiences, similar yet dissimilar. There is a perpetual slipping-back, then a going-forward."[19] Through his close contact with Whitman's poetry while writing the *Meditations*, Roethke discovered the ideal word to describe the back-and-forth motion that he finds characteristic of all journeys. "To rock," as it is used by Whitman in "Out of the Cradle Endlessly Rocking" to describe the movement of all living beings through birth into life and thence from life

19 "Open Letter," *On the Poet and His Craft*, p. 39.

into death, becomes one of Roethke's essential verbs. By using the word in "I'm Here," he introduces another echo of Whitman into a poem already resounding with reverberations: "The body, delighting in thresholds,/Rocks in and out of itself." At the end of the last *Meditation*, the old woman says, "The wind rocks with my wish" and

> I rock in my own dark,
> Thinking, God has need of me.
> The dead love the unborn.
> (CP 172)

This "rocking" movement is inherent even in the structure of single lines: "Do these bones live? Can I live with these bones?" When the old woman utters these words, she seems to be asking rather practical questions about her aged condition and wondering how she can sustain life in her time-worn body. But through implicit references to the Bible ("Can these bones live?" Ezekiel 37:3) and to Eliot ("Shall these bones live?" "Ash-Wednesday," part II), Roethke's "Do these bones live?" becomes a question not only about the body but about the soul, not only about this life but about death and future life. The old woman wishes to be set free from the senses and from reason and to have the faith of Ezekiel and of the speaker in Eliot's poem, whose "bones sang chirping": "O to be delivered from the rational into the realm of pure song" ("What Can I Tell My Bones?" part 2).

In "Song of the Open Road," Whitman describes "old age" as "Calm, expanded, broad" and as "flowing free with the delicious near-by freedom of death." Such finally is the old age of Roethke's protagonist. She is "calm": "I'm released from the dreary dance of opposites." Her life is "expanded": "I stretch in all directions." And if not exactly "broad," she is at least thick: "I'm thick with leaves." She has that same Whitmanesque sense of freedom. "I take the liberties a short life permits," she says.

An early version of the "Fourth Meditation" contained the following passage:

> Suffering may be permanent and obscure,
> And dark hang on the waters of the soul.[20]

The lines are from Wordsworth's tragedy *The Borderers*:

> Suffering is permanent, obscure, and dark,
> And shares the nature of infinity.
> (Act III, lines 409-410)

Roethke wrote in a letter in 1956 that the old woman "makes references . . . to old bore, Wordsworth."[21] In the final version of the poem these lines were deleted. Roethke may have decided that in this instance Wordsworth's voice, like Tiresome Tom's, was weary and drained, and it was instead in Whitman that he discovered a voice both aged and energetic. Like Blake's voice of the Ancient Bard but unlike Eliot's Gerontion, Whitman's constant mask as prophet of the new world preserves in the face of time those youthful energies which Roethke is now asking of his tradition. Significantly, it is a tradition in American verse, thus containing within itself an oxymoronic construct where past, present, and future all merge.

[20] Theodore Roethke Collection, University of Washington, Seattle (Literary Manuscripts, Poetry, D-Fo, Box 19).

[21] *Selected Letters*, p. 211.

VII

A Storm of Correspondences

In *Meditations of an Old Woman* (1958), Roethke clearly expands his sense of tradition. He places his poems within the context of two genres—the dramatic monologue and the meditation—and brings together a creative and critical gathering of three poets (Whitman, Eliot, Roethke) whereby we are asked to read each poet through the perspective provided by the others. In the *Mixed Sequence* (from *The Far Field*, 1964), we do not find a further development of these complex relationships or the discovery and assimilation of new poets. Rather we have a reprise—a reinvestigation of poets Roethke had earlier made part of his tradition. Along with the radical developments of the *North American Sequence* and *Sequence, Sometimes Metaphysical*, Roethke strengthens the sense of his own past by re-echoing some of the writers to whom he was particularly attracted. Roethke's final elegy, for his Aunt Tilly, has the selfsame source as one of his earlier elegies, "Frau Bauman, Frau Schmidt, and Frau Schwartze."[1] The description of the old women who worked in the greenhouses begins on an almost purely naturalistic level:

> Gone the three ancient ladies
> Who creaked on the greenhouse ladders,
> Reaching up white strings
> To wind, to wind

[1] "Frau Bauman, Frau Schmidt, and Frau Schwartze" was first published in the *New Yorker*, No. 28 (March 29, 1952), p. 38. With the publication of *The Waking* (1953), this poem was added to the section of greenhouse poems, placed between "Old Florist" and "Transplanting."

The sweet-pea tendrils, the smilax,
Nasturtiums, the climbing
Roses, to straighten
Carnations, red
Chrysanthemums; the stiff
Stems, jointed like corn,
They tied and tucked,—
These nurses of nobody else.

As the poem continues, however, supernatural powers are attributed to the crones:

Quicker than birds, they dipped
Up and sifted the dirt;
They sprinkled and shook;
They stood astride pipes,
Their skirts billowing out wide into tents,
Their hands twinkling with wet;
Like witches they flew along rows
Keeping creation at ease;
With a tendril for needle
They sewed up the air with a stem;
They teased out the seed that the cold kept
    asleep,—
All the coils, loops, and whorls.
They trellised the sun; they plotted for more
    than themselves.

The "three ancient ladies" have become the three Fates, with the power of life and death over a part of creation. They are the Parcae of the plants. The verbal echoes from Yeats's "Lines Written in Dejection" suggest that Frau Bauman, Frau Schmidt, and Frau Schwartze are part real, part imaginary:

All the wild witches, those most noble ladies,
For all their broom-sticks and their tears,
Their angry tears, are gone.
("Lines Written in Dejection")

Gone the three ancient ladies. . . .
Like witches they flew along rows . . .
("Frau Bauman, Frau Schmidt,
and Frau Schwartze")

In the last few lines of the poem Roethke further extends the mythic qualities of his characters by directing the reader to another of Yeats's poems, "The Magi":

Now, when I'm alone and cold in my bed,
They still hover over me,
These ancient leathery crones,
With their bandannas stiffened with sweat,
And their thorn-bitten wrists,
And their snuff-laden breath blowing lightly over
me in my first sleep.
("Frau Bauman, Frau Schmidt,
and Frau Schwartze")

Now as at all times I can see in the mind's eye,
In their stiff, painted clothes, the pale,
unsatisfied ones . . .
With all their ancient faces like rain-beaten
stones,
And all their helms of silver hovering side by side,
And all their eyes still fixed . . .
("The Magi")[2]

Roethke invests his "three ancient ladies" with that archetypal dimension of being possessed by Yeats's three wise men. The word *still* in both passages suggests that the figures are eternal—in Yeats's poem because they are transformed into artifacts, in Roethke's because they are a permanent part of his memory, both personal and literary.

In his later "Elegy" Roethke wishes to present the mutability of human life while at the same time showing that there are certain eternal qualities in the personality. Thus he

[2] *The Collected Poems of W. B. Yeats*, p. 124.

begins his poem by returning to "The Magi" for Yeats's image which conveys at once decay and permanence, ". . . faces like rain-beaten stones":

> Her face like a rain-beaten stone on the day she
> rolled off
> With the dark hearse, and enough flowers for an
> alderman,—
> And so she was, in her way, Aunt Tilly.
>
> (CP 223)[3]

Among the best poems in the *Mixed Sequence* are those in which Roethke focuses his thought on a single animal or flower—on, for instance, a meadow mouse:

> In a shoe box stuffed in an old nylon stocking
> Sleeps the baby mouse I found in the meadow,
> Where he trembled and shook beneath a stick
> Till I caught him up by the tail and brought
> him in,
> Cradled in my hand,
> A little quaker, the whole body of him trembling,
> His absurd whiskers sticking out like a
> cartoon-mouse,

[3] Also, at the end of "Elegy" compare Aunt Tilly's "Two steady eyes" with the "eyes still fixed" in "The Magi." Roethke's "celestial supermarket" is clearly not part of Yeats's idiom. It very likely has its source in Allen Ginsberg's "A Supermarket in California," *Howl and Other Poems* (San Francisco: City Lights, 1956), p. 23.

"In my hungry fatigue, and shopping for images, I went into the neon fruit supermarket. . . .

"I saw you, Walt Whitman, childless, lonely old grubber, poking among the meats in the refrigerator and eyeing the grocery boys."

(Ginsberg)

> I see you in some celestial supermarket,
> Moving serenely among the leeks and cabbages,
> Probing the squash,
> Bearing down, with two steady eyes,
> On the quaking butcher.
>
> (Roethke)

Roethke, too, was "shopping for images."

His feet like small leaves,
Little lizard-feet,
Whitish and spread wide when he tried to
struggle away,
Wriggling like a miniscule puppy. . . .
("The Meadow Mouse," CP 227)

According to Allan Seager, "Ted once went out into the field near his house. He went out and found a field mouse and brought it into the house exactly as he tells in the poem. This, his wife said, was perfectly true."[4] But, as we have seen, there is no separation in Roethke's sensibility between reading and experience, and thus "The Meadow Mouse," like so many of his poems, is a blending of literary with personal memory. The immediate subject comes from his own experience; the way of looking at and writing about that experience is the result of his admiration for D. H. Lawrence's poems in *Birds, Beasts, and Flowers.* Roethke's "baby mouse," which he calls "my thumb of a child that nuzzled in my palm," is surely related to Lawrence's "baby tortoise" who was "no bigger than my thumbnail."[5] A comparison of just a few lines from "Snake" with "The Meadow Mouse" reveals the impact which Lawrence's language and rhythms had upon Roethke:

How glad I was he had come like a guest in quiet,
to drink at my water-trough . . .

Was it humility to feel so honoured?
I felt so honoured.

("Snake")

Now he's eaten his three kinds of cheese and drunk
from his bottle-cap watering-trough— . . .

[4] "An Evening with Ted Roethke," *Michigan Quarterly*, 6, no. 4 (Fall, 1967), 242. The three participants in this discussion were Allan Seager, Stanley Kunitz, and John Ciardi.

[5] *The Complete Poems of D. H. Lawrence*, ed. Vivian de Sola Pinto and Warren Roberts (New York: Viking Press, 1964), p. 353.

Do I imagine he no longer trembles
When I come close to him?
He seems no longer to tremble.
("The Meadow Mouse")

Roethke learned from Lawrence how to make the reader forget the poet entirely and see only the creature. Compare their detailed descriptions of animals sunning themselves. Lawrence's lion

. . . lay in the mouth of a cave
And sunned his whiskers,
And lashed his tail slowly, slowly . . .

But later, in the sun of the afternoon,
Having tasted all there was to taste, and having
slept his fill
He fell to frowning, as he lay with his head on
his paws
And the sun coming in through the narrowest fibril
of a slit in his eyes.
("St Mark")

Roethke's lizard also

. . . has eaten well—
I can see that by the distended pulsing middle;
And his world and mine are the same,
The Mediterranean sun shining on us, equally,
His head, stiff as a scarab, turned to one side,
His right eye staring straight at me,
One leaf-like foot hung laxly
Over the worn curb of the terrace,
The tail straight as an awl,
Then suddenly flung up and over,
Ending curled around and over again,
A thread-like firmness.
("The Lizard," CP 226)

Lawrence wrote in his "Lizard" that "If men were as much men as lizards are lizards,/they'd be worth looking at." Since each lizard is no different in appearance or behavior from any other one, each is the perfect expression of his species. But each man is highly individualized and therefore, according to Lawrence, is a deviation from the basic pattern of maleness. Roethke, like Lawrence, purposely confuses the individual with the class in his "The Lizard," which ends,

> To whom does this terrace belong?—.
> With its limestone crumbling into fine greyish
>   dust,
> Its bevy of bees, and its wind-beaten rickety
>   sun-chairs.
> Not to me, but this lizard,
> Older than I, or the cockroach.

By seeing the entire species in the single lizard, the poet gains contact with an immortal form of life extending far back into the past and presumably into the future.

Roethke borrows and yet modifies some of Lawrence's most characteristic technical devices. To describe a "pike," for example, both poets employ the continuing triad, but Roethke reverses the movement of Lawrence's description by successively shortening rather than lengthening the lines.

> I saw, dimly,
> Once a big pike rush,
> And small fish fly like splinters.
>   (Lawrence, "Fish")

> With one sinuous ripple, then a rush,
> A thrashing-up of the whole pool,
> The pike strikes.
>   (Roethke, "The Pike")

In addition to poems on fish, reptiles, and animals, the *Mixed Sequence* also contains a poem on a flower, "The

Geranium." "Here," writes John Ciardi, Roethke "makes the geranium almost a beloved. He says, 'When I put her out once, by the garbage pail,' and he doesn't mean his wife, he means a geranium plant that he's describing. As far as I know, he's the only man in English poetry who refers to a geranium as 'her.'"[6] But Roethke's use of the feminine pronoun may have been suggested by Lawrence's line, "As if the redness of a red geranium could be anything but a sensual experience" ("Red Geranium and Godly Mignonette"). Roethke, like Lawrence, transforms his relationship with the geranium into a comically sensual experience, but ends, again like Lawrence, having somehow saved the traditional sentimentality of a "flower poem" by burlesquing it. Even in these animal and flower poems, where his attentions are concentrated on a natural object, Roethke still feels the necessity of being in touch with a poet in his tradition.

In the prose writings about his childhood, Roethke often describes his Prussian father's "love for order and discipline."[7] Thus, when he dedicates a poem to him, he does not employ the free verse patterns of Lawrence, but echoes the cadences of the one modern poet who never wrote a "loose" line in his life—Robert Frost. The second stanza of "Otto" is an instance of thorough assimilation: without borrowing from any specific poem, Roethke writes as if he were Frost:

> Once when he saw two poachers on his land,
> He threw his rifle over with one hand;
> Dry bark flew in their faces from his shot,—
> He always knew what he was aiming at.
> They stood there with their guns; he walked
> toward,
> Without his rifle, and slapped each one hard;

[6] "An Evening with Ted Roethke," p. 241.

[7] From *Selected Letters*, p. 162. See also "An American Poet Introduces Himself," *On the Poet and His Craft*, p. 8.

It was no random act, for those two men
Had slaughtered game, and cut young fir trees
down.
I was no more than seven at the time.
(CP 224)

Through Frost's idiom, his seemingly casual observations, and his woodland imagery, Roethke reveals his father as that particular type of character expressly portrayed in *North of Boston*—a straightforward, hard-working man with a quiet wisdom far deeper than that of more articulate men.

In the last stanza of "Otto" the death of the father is conceived of as a loss of the whole world of childhood and innocence. It is primarily Dylan Thomas who helped Roethke to give utterance to his sorrow. The predominant sound in the last stanza of both "Otto" and Thomas' "Fern Hill" is the diphthongal "ay." This sound is the Greek, as well as Spanish and other languages', cry of woe and can be considered as a linguistic equivalent of human lamentation. The emphatic repetition of "ay" adds to the meaning of both final stanzas with their moods of nostalgic longing. Roethke also borrows the diction and perspective of "Fern Hill." Thomas wakes to the realization that he now lives in a "childless land" forever distant from the enchanted farm of youth. Similarly, Roethke watches "the waking" of his "father's world" and feels the growing distance between his adult consciousness and the magical landscape of childhood.

One way of extending a tradition is to bring other poets into it, but in the *Mixed Sequence* we see Roethke deepening his tradition by discovering new resources in poets with whom he has been long familiar. The two decisive sections in *The Far Field* are the *North American Sequence* and *Sequence, Sometimes Metaphysical*. The first series is a journey through our continent, from its center to its western boundary. As Roethke moves from his own beginnings in the

Midwest to the Pacific Northwest, he considers the means by which a poet can come to know and join with the natural images he meets (and makes) along the way. In his travels he finds not only places but companions—those other poets who have also journeyed from interior to periphery and back again. He gives us a journey in space that is at once both personal and profoundly historical, and a journey in time that is both a reminiscence and a critique of literary tradition.

"The Longing" begins the sequence and establishes the themes, the images, and the tradition of poets upon which all of the other poems are developed. By assimilating phrases from other writers into his own work, Roethke directs the reader toward the tradition in which the poems participate and which they, in effect, reanimate. We must not neglect these subtle directives; for meaning is dependent on context, and the borrowed expressions make the works of others part of the total context of Roethke's poems. In "The Longing," the key phrase pointing out the way for the reader is "sunless sea," unmistakably reminding him of Coleridge. Although the image is from "Kubla Khan," it is primarily "Dejection: An Ode" that stands behind Roethke's poem.

In "Dejection" Coleridge recognizes the power and joy in Wordsworth's imaginative abilities and blesses him for them, but he also realizes and expresses in his ode his own inability (albeit not absolute) to participate in the interplay between man and nature found at the heart of Wordsworth's poetry. Roethke enters into this dialogue by answering Coleridge's "Dejection." "The Longing"—which, like Coleridge's poem, is an English ode—begins with a description of the same despair both within and without that characterizes Coleridge's psychological state in "Dejection":

On things asleep, no balm:
A kingdom of stinks and sighs,
Fetor of cockroaches, dead fish, petroleum,

Worse than castoreum of mink or weasels,
Saliva dripping from warm microphones,
Agony of crucifixion on barstools.
        Less and less the illuminated lips,
        Hands active, eyes cherished;
        Happiness left to dogs and children—
        (Matters only a saint mentions!)
Lust fatigues the soul.
How to transcend this sensual emptiness?
(Dreams drain the spirit if we dream too long.)
In a bleak time, when a week of rain is a year,
The slag-heaps fume at the edge of the raw cities:
The gulls wheel over their singular garbage;
The great trees no longer shimmer;
Not even the soot dances.

(CP 187)

"How to transcend this sensual emptiness?" basically means "How does one get beyond this state of physicality?" But if we link this line with Coleridge's descriptions of the way in which he senses nature and yet does not "feel" its influence upon his mind, we see that Roethke's "sensual emptiness" similarly suggests a poverty of the imagination. Both poets lament the failure of their creative powers:

> And still I gaze—and with how blank an eye! . . .
> My genial spirits fail.
>
> ("Dejection: An Ode," lines 30, 39)

> And the spirit fails to move forward, . . .
> An eyeless starer.
>
> ("The Longing," 1)

Coleridge saw the imagination as a force that can project mind into nature and impart significance to both; however, in the ode his "genial spirits," those shaping energies which move forward into the world around him, have ceased to transform that world. Like Coleridge's, Roethke's physical senses respond to his environment, but those imaginative faculties that discover and create organic metaphors falter. Both poets figure the reality of their dejection as a "dark dream" ("Dejection," line 95; "The Longing," line 28) that must be transmuted into a vision that exceeds despair. Just as the "crescent moon" in Coleridge's ode is taken as an emblem for the end of one cycle and the beginning of another, "the moon" that "could pare itself so thin" in Roethke's ode marks a major division in the images of that poem. Roethke begins to move away from despondency into renewed creative powers, and away from Coleridge to Wordsworth and Whitman. He conceives of the image from Coleridge's "Kubla Khan" as a symbol for the psychological conditions explored in "Dejection" and suggests that the imaginative powers can be seen to spring up from this "sunless sea," this dark and undifferentiated world described in the first section of "The Longing": "A great flame rises from the sunless sea" ("The Longing," Part II).

Part III is built stylistically and rhythmically as an interlude modeled on Whitman's characteristic devices, with a series of self-contained lines, each beginning with the first person pronoun. Recalling Whitman's "I would raise my voice jocund and strong with reference to consummations,"[8] Roethke begins

> I would with the fish, the blackening salmon,
> and the mad lemmings,
> The children dancing, the flowers widening. . . .
> I would unlearn the lingo of exasperation, all
> the distortions of malice and hatred;
> I would believe my pain: and the eye quiet on
> the growing rose;
> I would delight in my hands, the branch singing,
> altering the excessive bird; . . .
> I would be a stream, winding between great
> striated rocks in late summer. . . .
>
> (CP 188)

[8] The line is from Whitman's "So Long!"

Roethke turns his attention away from the "microphones" and "barstools" and, as does Whitman in many of his poems, focuses upon the multiplicity of life forms in nature. His plea to be one with the creatures is in sharp contrast to that Coleridgean alienation between self and environment dealt with in the first two sections of the poem. Again like Whitman, who accepted death as part of life and as part of his poetry, Roethke does not try to deny the role that death plays in the cycle of life, but he now wishes to accept even the decay presented in the initial lines of the poem as important to the total experience that can be transformed into poetry. By turning to Whitman, he indeed "unlearns" in the course of this very poem "the lingo of exasperation."

By his acceptance of the physical activity of nature as a part of the self, Roethke hopes to achieve serenity, not through transcendence, but by penetrating inward. "I long for the imperishable quiet at the heart of form," he writes, echoing Wordsworth's descriptions of the same type of calm fulfillment in *The Excursion*: "The longing for confirmed tranquility,/Inward and outward . . . / Where earth is quiet" and ". . . central peace, subsisting at the heart/Of endless agitation" (Book III, 398-399, 401; Book IV, 1146-1147).[9] Roethke may well have discovered the title for his poem in the first quotation.

The poet has been spiritually refreshed, but he still has the rest of the journey of his mortal life to pursue. The poem ends

> Old men should be explorers?
> I'll be an Indian.
> Ogalala?
> Iroquois.
>
> (CP 189)[10]

[9] Roethke was of course familiar with Book IV of *The Excursion*, since one of his earlier poems "Bring the Day!" (CP 77) takes its title from Wordsworth's poem.

[10] In the first edition of *The Far Field* (New York: Doubleday, 1964), the word *Ogalala* does not appear in "The Longing."

In one of his earlier sequences, *Meditations of an Old Woman*, Roethke explored the close connections between Whitman and Eliot; and it is not surprising that as he begins "to move forward" to make his journey into the self, which, as in Whitman's "Song of Myself," is also a journey through America, he borrows an appropriate line from Part v of Eliot's "East Coker," "Old men ought to be explorers." Even the movement from Eliot to "an Indian" may have been suggested by Roethke's reading, for at the beginning of S. Musgrove's book *T. S. Eliot and Walt Whitman*, with which Roethke was thoroughly familiar, is the following chapter heading:

T. S. ELIOT AND WALT WHITMAN

. . . the unknown
Apostle of the Indians, Eliot . . .
—H. W. Longfellow, *Eliot's Oak*

> . . . the most individual parts of (a poet's) work may be those in which the dead poets, his ancestors, assert their immortality most vigorously.
>
> —T. S. Eliot, *Tradition and the Individual Talent*[11]

While the first short epigraph influenced the ending of Roethke's "The Longing," it is the second epigraph that perfectly explains the function of such influence in the creation of the poem.

Eliot pervasively affects the whole of the *North American Sequence*. Roethke's "Journey to the Interior" is filled with verbal and rhythmic echoes of Eliot's "Journey of the Magi." Like Eliot, Roethke varies the line length to make the long lines seem even longer and slower and to make the short ones seem shorter and more pointed. The matter-of-fact tone of "Journey of the Magi" is paralleled by the apparent

[11] Musgrove's work was published in Wellington, New Zealand, in 1952, just before Roethke began writing his *Meditations of an Old Woman*, and it played an important role in Roethke's use of Whitman's and Eliot's techniques (see Chapter VI).

literalness of Roethke's journey as he carefully describes natural objects rather than directly describing psychological events. In each poem the poet provides a key to the real subject in his title.

More prevalent and central than the echoes in vocabulary or rhythm are the imagistic and thematic similarities between Roethke and Eliot. This influence, primarily of "Ash-Wednesday" and the *Four Quartets*, those two works which Roethke copied out in longhand again and again,[12] permeates every poem in the *North American Sequence*. Roethke's "Meditation at Oyster River" follows the basic outlines of a religious meditation: it begins with a composition of place and continues this composition throughout most of its lines.[13] Just as the devout meditator concentrates with all of his powers on individual objects (the nail in Christ's right hand, the spear thrusting into His side), so too Roethke focuses his eye on particulars within the silence of the contemplative condition. Part of the meditative tradition in religious poetry is that the meditator not only comes to understand the object of his thought but also becomes one with it. Or, as Roethke writes, following a catalogue of natural creatures, "With these I would be." The meditator struggles out of division into union. In the third and fourth parts of "Meditation at Oyster River" Roethke concentrates upon the moving waters of a river thawing in the early spring and then identifies his own psychological movement in this poem with the river:

> Water's my will, and my way,
> And the spirit runs, intermittently,
> In and out of the small waves.
>
> (CP 191-192)

[12] Theodore Roethke Collection, University of Washington, Seattle (Other Poets in Theodore Roethke's Hand, A-R, Box 63).

[13] I am here defining Roethke's and Eliot's use of the meditative tradition in English poetry as set forth in Louis L. Martz, *The Poetry of Meditation: A Study in English Religious Literature*.

Roethke, however, is not one with the animals; he only wishes to be. And the spirit is only "intermittently" one with the water. Yet the tentative quality of these images is not enough to prepare us for the image of division that concludes the poem:

In the first of the moon,
All's a scattering,
A shining.

This unexpected turn is difficult to account for as part of the traditional pattern of the meditative poem, but we can find both precedent and source for it in Eliot's meditation, "Ash-Wednesday":

Under a juniper-tree the bones sang,
scattered and shining.

In this second section of "Ash-Wednesday," as in the second poem of Roethke's *North American Sequence*, the dialectic of division and union reaches a temporary synthesis wherein the light of revelation that comes at the end of a meditation is partly achieved. In both poems it is not a light from within, but a reflected light, and in Roethke's poem the light is doubly reflected. "I shift on my rock," Roethke writes, for he has only begun his journey out of the single self and towards "the imperishable quiet at the heart of form" ("The Longing") that Eliot also asks for at the end of "Ash-Wednesday":

Teach us to sit still
Even among these rocks.

Like all good Christian meditations, Eliot's poems have as their goal an understanding and finally a love of God. Roethke's poems are also in the meditative tradition and he too reaches for understanding and love, but, within this basic similarity, obvious distinctions appear. Eliot is pervasively religious, even theological, in his interests, and thus he finally must move from the physical world and the imagery of that world to a spiritual world in which abstract concepts replace images from nature. For Eliot, basic questions about love, time, and space can find their ultimate answers only on this higher level. Roethke is never so willing to desert the natural world: these same questions are answered not by leaving the woods and the waters but by penetrating more deeply into their interiors. As Roethke writes in "The Far Field," "What I love is near at hand./ Always in earth and air." And, again, in "The Rose," "What need for heaven, then,/With that man, and those roses?" Here, then, is the great difference within the pattern of similarities. For Eliot, "Words . . . crack and sometimes break" ("Burnt Norton"), but for Roethke, "ice . . . begins cracking and . . . breaks away" ("Meditation at Oyster River"). It is in the act of creating organic metaphors, and not in Eliot's pursuit of abstractions, that Roethke finds salvation.

"The Rose" begins, "There are those to whom place is unimportant" (CP 202). But this certainly does not include Roethke or Eliot. The sense of place shared by the *North American Sequence* and the *Four Quartets* reaches beyond its composition within a meditation. Just as each of the Quartets takes its title from a particular location, so also Roethke's poems echo with place names: the Bullhead, the Dakotas, Oyster River, Michigan, the Tittebawasee, the Tombstone. For both poets these places have a double significance—the locations have personal and historic meaning. The names in Eliot describe a journey from the Middle West (the Mississippi River, "the strong brown god" of "The Dry Salvages") to New England (the Dry Salvages off the coast of Massachusetts) and finally to England (Burnt Norton, East Coker, and Little Gidding). Roethke moves west rather than east, from Michigan to the Dakotas and the Rockies and finally to the Pacific Northwest. These east and west journeys recall the physical movement of each poet's life, but in their poems the cardinal concern is with a movement in the other direction, back from where they are to where they came from—the Midwest. These journeys into the interior—both of the self and of the continent—have a temporal as well as spatial dimension.

Indeed both the *Four Quartets* and the *North American Sequence* are notable for their embodiment of the space-time continuum. For Eliot and Roethke the sense and identification of place are a stimulus to the memory as it moves back and forth from past to present and finally brings them both to one. Eliot, for example, returns to East Coker, the ancestral home of his family. By journeying away from his home in America, he has come to a "home" in a profounder sense and found that "in my end is my beginning." In the last poem of the *North American Sequence* Roethke stands on the Pacific shore. He moves back in time in the second section of the poem to the greenhouses of Michigan and his youth. Linking past and present, Midwest and Northwest, is the crucial image of the rose. It is indeed a hybrid rose, like his father's "elaborate hybrids," not only bringing together present ("this rose, this rose in the sea-wind") and past ("roses, roses,/White and red, in the wide six-hundred-foot greenhouses"), but also bringing the present poet (Roethke) into immediate contact with his tradition. Roethke recaptures the past through his meditation of the rose, just as Eliot tries to redeem the past in the rose-garden. Eliot's "single Rose" ("Ash-Wednesday," II) may be the primary source for Roethke's "single wild rose," but of course the image resounds throughout Western literature back to Dante. Eliot and Roethke search for ways to overcome the discontinuity of past and present, and, at least in their poetry, they redeem time by joining their own voices with earlier voices.

Within the journey and within the rose is a point that has as its temporal dimension eternity and as its spatial dimension infinity. Eliot speaks of this point in terms of time when he writes, "Only through time time is conquered" ("Burnt Norton," II). Roethke makes the same statement in terms of space: "All finite things reveal infinitude" ("The Far

Field"). Both poets find solace, if not ultimate fulfillment, within a perception of the moment that reveals the eternal and in a union with things beyond the self that expand that self to give a glimpse of infinity. Roethke writes,

> I came upon the true ease of myself,
> As if another man appeared out of the depths of my
> being,
> And I stood outside myself,
> Beyond becoming and perishing.
> ("The Rose," CP 205)

The title *Sequence, Sometimes Metaphysical* directs us toward both a mode of philosophical speculation and a school of seventeenth-century poetry. The content of the poems in this group follows the tradition of philosophy that investigates the essential reality beyond physical appearances; the structure of the poems follows that tradition of poetry which in the twentieth century has been most often characterized as "metaphysical." Many individual lines from "In a Dark Time" point to both traditions. "A steady storm of correspondences," for example, refers both to those systems of analogy between the spiritual and the physical—most marked in symbolist poetry—that play a key role in many forms of metaphysical speculation and also to that system of correspondences upon which the conceit is based. "All natural shapes blazing unnatural light" suggests that forms in nature, when properly perceived, reveal spiritual (i.e., "unnatural") realities and, further, that metaphysical verse can deal with spiritual questions through metaphors based upon "natural shapes" in the material world. Throughout the sequence Roethke investigates multiple correspondences between the outer world and the soul and looks into "natural shapes" to find their spiritual significance. When the "storm of correspondences" reaches its height, not only does he discover similarities between self and other, soul and body, but also, by transmuting nature into spirit through the penetrating imagination and thereby lifting himself out of the limitations of the isolated personality, he discovers in "Once More, the Round," the final poem in the series, that "everything comes to One."

In the first stanza of "In Evening Air," Roethke again directs us to the kind of structures of thought that he will be using in his sequence:

> A dark theme keeps me here,
> Though summer blazes in the vireo's eye.
> Who would be half possessed
> By his own nakedness?
> Waking's my care—
> I'll make a broken music, or I'll die.
> (CP 240)

The last line refers back to Elizabethan and seventeenth-century music, which was arranged to be played by several different instruments. Thus, oddly enough, "broken" has a meaning quite close to that of our modern word "concerted." Roethke will play several "instruments" at once by writing poems that deal simultaneously with both spirit and nature. Even individual words can have this same multivalence. "Nakedness" in the above lines must, of course, refer to a particular physical condition, but it also should be seen as a spiritual and psychological state. Henry Vaughan uses "nakedness" in the same double-sense when he describes men standing before God:

> Then comes the light! which when you spy,
> And see your nakedness thereby,
> Praise him who dealt his gifts so free
> In tears to you, in fire to me.[14]

[14] "Vain Wits and Eyes," *The Complete Poetry of Henry Vaughan*, p. 266. In a late notebook Roethke quotes a line from Vaughan's "Vanity of Spirit": "The little light I had was gone." A few pages later, Roethke writes his own line: "The little light I had was Henry Vaughan's." Theodore Roethke Collection (Notebooks, [1961]-[1963], Box 43, #210).

Vaughan means literally the physical nakedness of man when revealed in light and also the spiritual nakedness of the soul. Roethke, like Vaughan and other metaphysical poets, achieves a complexity of thought by concentrating several levels of meaning into one word.

Another figure that links several meanings together is metaphysical paranomasia. George Herbert's title "The Collar" refers primarily to the bond of conscience joining man to God. But by reading the last stanza, we realize that Herbert is combining together in his title other important themes:

> But as I rav'd and grew more fierce and wilde
> At every word,
> Me thoughts I heard one calling, Child!
> And I reply'd, My Lord.[15]

The title now refers to "choler" (the anger of the speaker) and "caller" (the voice of God), as well as to "collar." Roethke's title "I Waited" involves similar word play. The poem begins

> I waited for the wind to move the dust;
> But no wind came.
> I seemed to eat the air;
> The meadow insects made a level noise.
> I rose, a heavy bulk, above the field.
> (CP 247)

By the end of the first stanza, the title also means, "I, weighted."

The linking of opposites is another rhetorical device characteristic of both metaphysical poetry and Roethke's sequence. In "The Motion," for example, we find "This torment is my joy," "By striding, I remain," and "The close dirt dancing." At the end of "Infirmity" Roethke explains

[15] *The Works of George Herbert*, ed. F. E. Hutchinson (Oxford: Clarendon Press, 1951), pp. 153-154.

his purpose in employing these oxymoronic constructions—this joining of contraries results for him in an expansion and unification of the senses:

> When opposites come suddenly in place,
> I teach my eyes to hear, my ears to see . . .
> (CP 244)

Roethke is much concerned with modes of perception in these poems. The sequence begins, "In a dark time, the eye begins to see." Apparently he believed that all these "metaphysical" rhetorical techniques were more than just word games, for they open up new perspectives on the actual interrelationships between the self and the world. Finally, the devices of poetry become a means of discovery rather than just a method of communicating what is already known.

In much of Renaissance poetry, including metaphysical verse, natural objects become emblems of spiritual qualities. Roethke employs this emblematic method and in some poems even bases his imagery on traditional devices. "The Restored" is centered on a soul conceived of as a feminine creature with only one wing. Since the soul is bound to earth, it "can't fly" into more spiritual realms. Roethke's image is based upon the traditional emblem for this same condition of the soul in which it is pictured as a woman with a winged-hand reaching up to God but with her other hand weighted down to earth.[16] The movement from "the soul" to a "wind-tattered butterfly" in "The Motion" seems less of a sudden leap when we realize that the butterfly is a traditional device for the soul.[17] But even though these images function as emblems, they are kept within a context of naturalistic description that they do not have in Renais-

[16] See Alciati's Emblem 121. See also Geffrey Whitney, *A Choice of Emblemes* (Leyden, 1586), p. 152. This is one of the most common devices found throughout Renaissance emblem books.

[17] The traditional butterfly emblem is pictured and explained in Jacob Bryant, *A New System, or, an Analysis of Ancient Mythology* (London, 1774-1776), II, plate 10.

sance emblem books. Nature is invested by Roethke with the significance of symbol, but it does not thereby become merely a landscape of abstract hieroglyphs.

Perhaps Roethke's sequence should be related to several genres of seventeenth-century verse, rather than just to the metaphysical. His villanelle, "The Right Thing," is in the *beatus vir* tradition that began with Latin eclogues and became a popular motif in Renaissance and seventeenth-century poetry. One of the major English examples is Ben Jonson's "To Sir Robert Wroth." In *The Happy Man*, Maren-Sofie Røstvig writes that, "Despite its obvious indebtedness to classical sources [mainly to *Georgics*, II], Ben Jonson's poem is more than a mere imitation. The English poet has succeeded in stamping this elaborate poetic compliment with his own genius. There is fire and vigor even in the lines where the indebtedness is most obvious: 'Let others watch in guiltie armes, and stand the fire of a rash command. . . .' "[18] Roethke's poem begins

> Let others probe the mystery if they can.
> Time-harried prisoners of *Shall* and *Will*—
> The right thing happens to the happy man.
>
> The bird flies out, the bird flies back again;
> The hill becomes the valley, and is still;
> Let others delve that mystery if they can.
>
> (CP 250)

Roethke draws upon Jonson just as Jonson drew upon the classics, both realizing, as Roethke said, that "imitation, conscious imitation, is one of the great methods, perhaps *the* method of learning to write."[19] In his *beatus ille* poem Roethke ceases to probe into the metaphysical basis of being and acknowledges and accepts "the mystery."

[18] Maren-Sofie Røstvig, *The Happy Man: Studies in the Metamorphoses of a Classical Ideal*, revised edition (Oslo: Norwegian Universities Press, 1962), p. 64.

[19] "How to Write Like Somebody Else," *On the Poet and His Craft*, p. 69.

Afterword

Just as Roethke related his poems to specific works rather than to abstract concepts of style, he saw his literary tradition not as a series of periods but as a community of selected individual talents, somehow in touch with one another even as he was in touch with them. At first this group was limited mainly to a few women poets whom he admired, but the circle widened rapidly as he reached out to Wordsworth, Blake, and Smart, to several Renaissance poets, including Donne and Sir John Davies, to the great moderns, Whitman, Yeats, and Eliot, and finally even to a medieval poet, Dante. In spite of Roethke's apparent eclecticism, many important figures in English literature were never invited into his tradition. The Neo-classical poets of the Restoration and first half of the eighteenth century, Milton, Shelley, and the Victorians are all absent.

The creation of this community began as a conscious effort of imitation and was dependent upon a high level of insight into the meaning and structures of each poem from which he borrowed phrases and images. But as Roethke created his tradition, he was created by it, and in his later poetry his use of the past became virtually subconscious. The techniques and images learned over many years of reading became as much a part of his memory as his personal non-literary experience, so that eventually there was no division in his mind between the two. When writing his later poems, Roethke may well have forgotten the original literary source for a particular image or stylistic technique, and in this way imitation became, for him, one with invention. Overstating the case more than I would do, Roethke wrote in one of his late notebooks, "I have no mind at all: I just remember."[1] Finally, then, his sense of tradition encompassed not only a conscious historical attitude, but a psychological state, and his act of imitation was not a mechanical process, but a basic component of those imaginative faculties most directly involved in the creation of a poem. The degree to which his sense of tradition was an emotional attitude involving his whole psychological condition is most clearly demonstrated in his belief that while he was writing "The Dance" Yeats was in his presence.[2]

The strongest single influence on Roethke's concept of his tradition, and one of the most important poets in that tradition, is T. S. Eliot. The few explicit critical statements that Roethke makes in his essays are based on Eliot's own; and his community of poets, living and dead, grows out of Eliot's "conception of poetry as a living whole of all the poetry that has ever been written."[3] In fact, most of the poets in Roethke's sodality, with the major exception of Wordsworth, are those same figures to whom Eliot was most attracted and whom he was most responsible for drawing attention to in this century. Those two influential English poets, Milton and Shelley, excluded from Eliot's tradition, are also notably absent from Roethke's. Regardless of the value for the critic of Eliot's concept of tradition, Roethke proves its value for the creator. The one major difference between the attitudes of these two twentieth-century poets towards their literary forebears is that Eliot felt the need for a body of criticism to structure rigorously that tradition of poetry to which the modern poet should attempt to make his own contribution; whereas Roethke connected himself with a less carefully defined and hierarchical association of poets.

Roethke offers in his poems a number of metaphors mark-

[1] Theodore Roethke Collection, University of Washington, Seattle (Notebooks, [1961]-[1963], Box 43, #210).

[2] See "On 'Identity,'" *On the Poet and His Craft*, p. 24. Also see my commentary on "Four for Sir John Davies," pp. 108-117.

[3] "Tradition and the Individual Talent," *Selected Essays*, p. 7.

ing his evolving conception of the relationship between "tradition and the individual talent." In his earliest book, the poetry of the past is viewed as an inherited burden. The pressure of the past is a sinister force against which the modern poet self-consciously struggles to assert his own originality. Later, Roethke begins to discover that a literary inheritance is not given as a birthright but must be created as a means for permitting the poet to realize his own abilities through imitation and finally assimilation—arts that at their worst are mimicry and blatant theft and at their best enable the poet to find "the accent" of his own speech[4] and yet at the same time to overcome the limitations of the solitary talent unsupported by tradition.

As early as *The Lost Son and Other Poems* (1948) Roethke was fascinated with the notion that "to go forward . . . it is necessary first to go back,"[5] and in the *Meditations of an Old Woman* (1958), Whitman's image of "rocking" became a metaphor for this back-and-forth movement of the poet as he responds to the past in order to move forward into new creations. In "Four for Sir John Davies," oscillation is harmonized into "the dance." Roethke borrowed this image from Davies and Yeats and transformed it into his final and most complex metaphor for the partnership of past and present poets. In "Once More, the Round," the last poem in his last volume, he wrote

> What's greater, Pebble or Pond?
> What can be known? The Unknown.
> My true self runs toward a Hill
> More! O More! visible.
>
> Now I adore my life
> With the Bird, the abiding Leaf,
> With the Fish, the questing Snail,

[4] "How to Write Like Somebody Else," *On the Poet and His Craft*, p. 66.

[5] "Open Letter," *On the Poet and His Craft*, p. 39.

And the Eye altering all;
And I dance with William Blake
For love, for Love's sake;

And everything comes to One,
As we dance on, dance on, dance on.
(CP 251)[6]

The eternal "Round" joins the partners into a single aesthetic whole—the poem itself. The temporal divisions separating the modern poet from his ancestors melt away. For Roethke, the present embodies the past, and, since the search for a tradition and the means by which it is defined are concomitant, the functions of the critic and the creator are the same.

Had Roethke lived longer, it is likely that his most important metaphors for his sense and use of tradition would have developed into something like myths. If he had enlarged his metaphor of "rocking" into a concept of history explaining the reanimation of the past in the present, it might well have been similar to Yeats's gyres. "The dance" in which "everything comes to One," if extended, might have become, like Blake's *Milton* and *Jerusalem*, an all-encompassing myth for the total assimilation of past into present poets and the realization of self through absorption into the organic structure of the poem.[7] Perhaps Roethke would have found the descent of Milton into the mind of Blake and the embrace of Creator and created at the end of *Jerusalem* prototypal myths for that process whereby the poet becomes his tradition and the tradition becomes the poet.

[6] The line "And the Eye altering all" is from Blake's "For the Eye altering alters all" in "The Mental Traveller," *Blake: Complete Writings*, p. 426.

[7] In "Theodore Roethke: The Power of Sympathy," *Theodore Roethke: Essays on the Poetry*, pp. 197-199, Roy Harvey Pearce suggests that if Roethke had lived longer, he might have written poems similar to Blake's prophecies. Thus Pearce's projection generally agrees with my speculations about the direction in which Roethke's concept of his tradition might have developed.

Index

Works cited, except Roethke's own, will be found under the author's name.

Abrams, M. H., 75, 76
"Abyss, The," 131
"Adamant, The," 11, 15, 16
Adams, Leonie, 20, 21, 23
Aeneas, 87, 88, 91
Alciati, Andrea, 162n
"American Poet Introduces Himself, An," 45, 46, 58, 148n
Ariosto, Ludovico, 25, 26
Arnold, Matthew, 87
"Auction, The," 10
Auden, W. H., 5; "As I Walked Out One Evening," 20
Augustine, St., 118, 122, 123
Austen, Jane, 126

"Ballad of the Clairvoyant Widow," 20
Baring-Gould, William S. and Ceil, 65, 77n
Bateson, F. W., 44, 45
Becquer, Gustavo, 122
Bennett, Joseph, 24n, 51n
Bentley, G. E., Jr., 92
Bible, 33n, 59, 91, 126, 132, 139
Bishop, John Peale, 9
Blackmur, R. P., 22
Blake, William, 6, 54-66, 69, 92-100, 105-107, 140, 165, 168; "Blossom, The," 61; *Book of Thel, The*, 4, 92, 93, 99, 100; "Ecchoing Green, The," 58; *For Children: The Gates of Paradise*, 56-58; *Four Zoas, The*, 90n, 97-100; "Holy Thursday," 60; *Island in the Moon, An*, 61, 66; *Jerusalem*, 61, 168; "Lamb, The," 57; "Laughing Song," 58; "Little Boy Found, The," 99, 100; "Little Boy Lost, The," 87, 88, 98-100; "Little Girl Found, The," 58; *Marriage of Heaven and Hell, The*, 90n, 93, 106; "Mental Traveller, The," 168n; *Milton*, 59, 77n, 168; "Nurse's Song," 58, 61; "Poison Tree, A," 63n; *Songs of Innocence and of Experience*, 57, 61, 62; "Spring," 58; *Visions of the Daughters of Albion*, 90n, 106
Bodkin, Maud, 84, 85, 88-90, 94, 103
Bogan, Louise, 18, 42, 108n
books owned by Roethke, 84, 86, 92, 109n, 119n, 120n
Botticelli, Sandro, 77-79
"Bring the Day!" 67-72, 80n, 83, 153n
Brittain, Robert, 51, 52
Bryant, Jacob, 162n
"Buds Now Stretch, The," 20, 21
Burke, Kenneth, 25, 104-106
Burns, Robert, 107

"Carnations," 34, 35
Cervantes, Miguel, 25
Chaucer, Geoffrey, 109
"Child on Top of a Greenhouse," 31-35
Ciardi, John, 145n, 148
Clare, John, 96
classroom procedures of Roethke, 5, 87n, 118n

Coleridge, Samuel Taylor, 107, 150-53; "Dejection: An Ode," 150-52; "Kubla Khan," 150, 152; "Rime of the Ancient Mariner, The," 89, 90, 94, 95, 100
Cowper, William, 76
"Cuttings (*later*)," 36

Damon, S. Foster, 60, 61, 77n, 98
Daniel, Samuel, 109
Dante, 6, 91, 114-16, 120, 127, 158, 165
Davie, Donald, 18
Davies, Sir John, 116, 165, 167; "Orchestra," 109-13
"Death Piece," 10, 11
De Quincey, Thomas, 40, 41
Dickinson, Emily, 13-16, 23, 43; "On this long storm," 14; "Our journey had advanced," 14; " 'Twas warm . . ." 15, 16
"Dolor," 37, 38
Donne, John, 117-19, 123-25, 165; "Dreame, The," 118; "Funerall, The," 19; "Loves Progress," 123; "Relique, The," 19
Donoghue, Denis, 126
Dostoevski, Feodor, 126
"Dream, The," 118-20
Drummond, William, 118, 119, 125
Dryden, John, 80

"Elegy," 5
"Elegy" (for Aunt Tilly), 141, 143, 144
Eliot, T. S., 3f, 21-24, 126-41, 154-58, 165, 166; "Ash-Wednesday," 38, 100, 130, 139, 155, 156, 158; "Burnt Norton," 101, 157, 158; "Dry Salvages, The," 129, 157; "East Coker," 101-103, 154, 157, 158; *Four Quartets*, 87, 100-103, 126, 136, 155, 157, 158; "Gerontion," 135, 140; "Journey of the Magi," 154, 155; "Little Gidding," 101, 132, 157; "Love Song of J. Alfred Prufrock, The," 37; "Metaphysical Poets, The," 79, 80; *Murder in the Cathedral*, 129; "Music of Poetry, The," 21, 22; *On Poetry and Poets*, 24; "Rock, The," 128; *Sacred Wood, The*, 5; "Song for Simeon, A," 135; *Sweeney Agonistes*, 74; "Tradition and the Individual Talent," 3, 22, 23, 154, 166; *Use of Poetry and the Use of Criticism, The*, 86, 87; "Waste Land, The," 11, 103
Emerson, Ralph Waldo, 49

Far Field, The, 141, 149, 153n
"Far Field, The," 6, 157-59
Fergusson, Francis, 25
"Feud," 7, 8
"First Meditation," 127, 133-38
"Flower Dump," 34
"Four for Sir John Davies," 109-17, 132, 166, 167
"Fourth Meditation," 129, 130, 137, 140
"Frau Bauman, Frau Schmidt, and Frau Schwartze," 141-43
Frazer, J. G., 29
Freud, Sigmund, 53, 54
Frost, Robert, 148, 149
Frye, Northrop, 88

"Geranium, The," 147, 148
Ginsberg, Allen, 144n
"Give Way, Ye Gates," 72-74, 80, 83
Graves, Robert, 20
Gray, Thomas, 6

Hamblen, Emily S., 92, 93
Hamlet, 87, 88
Handley-Taylor, Geoffrey, 66
Hartman, Geoffrey H., 25, 29
Hawthorne, Nathaniel, 8, 9
"Heard in a Violent Ward," 96
"Her Becoming," 129, 135

Herbert, George, 161
Herrick, Robert, 13, 22; "Vision, The," 73; "Wassaile, The," 72-74
Higginson, Thomas Wentworth, 14
Hobbes, Thomas, 75
Hogarth, William, 77n
Hopkins, Gerard Manley, 17, 18
"How to Write Like Somebody Else," 5, 19-22, 109, 131, 163, 167
Hugo, Victor, 60

"I Cry, Love! Love!" 90n, 106, 107
"I Knew a Woman," 120-23
"I Need, I Need," 56-59, 62, 63, 80n
"I Waited," 161
"I'm Here," 128, 130, 138, 139
"In a Dark Time," 159, 162
"In Evening Air," 160
"Infirmity," 161, 162
"Interlude," 11, 12

Janson, H. W., 123
Johnson, Samuel, 96, 97
Jonson, Ben, 22, 122, 125, 163
"Journey to the Interior," 154, 155
Joyce, James, 53n
Jung, C. G., 29, 53n, 84-89

Keats, John, 6
Kizer, Carolyn, 53n
Kunitz, Stanley, 22,84n, 85, 96n, 145n

Lawrence, D. H., 125, 134; *Birds, Beasts, and Flowers*, 145; "Fish," 147; "I Wish I Knew a Woman," 120; "Lizard," 147; *Rainbow, The*, 119, 120; "Red Geranium and Godly Mignonette," 148; "Snake," 145; "St Mark," 146
LETTERS OF ROETHKE, 9, 16, 18, 20, 43, 45, 86n, 95, 100, 104-106, 109, 112n, 127, 135, 136, 140, 148, 162
Lindenberger, Herbert, 25, 39n, 41n, 46n, 49
"Lines Upon Leaving a Sanitarium," 96, 97
"Lizard, The," 146, 147
"Long Alley, The," 93n
"'Long Live the Weeds,'" 17, 18
Longfellow, H. W., 60, 154
"Longing, The," 150-56
Lost Son and Other Poems, The, 3, 4, 24, 26, 29, 34, 36, 39, 138, 167
"Lost Son, The," 4, 46, 63, 66, 85-103
"Love's Progress," 123
Lowes, John Livingston, 113

Malkoff, Karl, 15, 28, 43, 44, 52, 53, 72, 74, 84n, 100, 101, 111n
Martin, Richard, 109
Martz, Louis L., 118, 134, 155n
Marvell, Andrew, 121, 125
"Meadow Mouse, The," 144-46
"Meditation at Oyster River," 155-57
"Meditation in Hydrotherapy," 96, 97
Meditations of an Old Woman, 5, 126-41, 154, 167
Meredith, William, 12, 13
"Mid-Country Blow," 11, 12
Miller, James E., Jr., 132, 133
Mills, Ralph J., Jr., 43, 52, 91, 111, 127, 136
Milton, John, 165, 166, 168; "At a Solemn Music," 80; "Lycidas," 77n
"Minimal, The," 36, 37, 90
Mixed Sequence, 141, 144, 147, 149
"Moss-Gathering," 25-29
Mother Goose, *see* nursery rhymes
"Motion, The," 161, 162
Musgrove, S., 127-35, 154

Nietzsche, 92, 93

"Night Crow," 41
"No Bird," 12-16, 134
North American Sequence, 141, 149-58
NOTEBOOKS AND MANUSCRIPTS OF ROETHKE, 32, 33, 59, 77n, 105n, 122, 127, 140, 155, 160, 165, 166
Nurmi, Martin K., 92
nursery rhymes, 60-67, 76, 77

"O Lull Me, Lull Me," 80-83
"O, Thou Opening, O," 60, 106, 107
Oedipus, 87
"Old Florist," 29-31, 141n
Olivero, Federico, 51, 52
"On 'Identity,'" 7, 9, 47, 79n, 89, 90, 92, 94, 107, 116, 117, 166
"On the Road to Woodlawn," 9, 10, 15, 17
"Once More, the Round," 5, 134, 135, 160, 167, 168
Open House, 7, 13, 24
"Open House," 10, 11, 17, 23
"Open Letter," 44-46, 52, 59, 60, 62, 85-87, 94, 99, 138, 167
Opie, Iona and Peter, 60n, 63-66
Orestes, 87
"Otto," 148, 149

Pearce, Roy Harvey, 53n, 100, 102, 168n
Picasso, Pablo, 123
"Pike, The," 147
"Plaint," 5
"Poetaster," 23
"Poetry of Louise Bogan, The," 42, 108
Pope, Alexander, 115, 116
"Praise," 18
Praise to the End!, 4, 43-51, 53n, 56, 80, 83-88, 103, 106
"Praise to the End!" 43, 63
"Prayer," 5
"Premonition, The," 18, 19
"Pure Fury, The," 124, 125

Ralegh, Sir Walter, 109, 116, 119
"Restored, The," 162
Richards, I. A., 122
"Right Thing, The," 163
Roethke, Helen Huebner (Roethke's mother), 126
Roethke, Otto (Roethke's father), 148, 149
ROETHKE, THEODORE, tradition, importance for understanding the poems, 3-6; childhood, 6, 25, 32, 43-46, 52, 54, 57-67, 98, 99, 148, 149; tradition, battle with, 7-23, 167; inability to write, 10-13; imitation of women poets, 13-23, 165; response to nature, 24-40, 68, 70, 72-74, 150-153; sexual overtones, 27, 28, 78; heroic figures, 25, 26, 30, 31, 87, 88, 112, 113; image of city, 37, 38; concepts of the imagination, 39-42, 86, 87, 113, 151, 152; oral poetry, 44, 45, 64; journey as metaphor, 46, 85-93, 115, 138, 150, 154, 155, 157, 158, 167; boat image, 47-49; music as metaphor, 52, 80-83, 110, 160; breakdown into dualities, 53-57, 98; concepts of sensibility, 74-80; archetypes, 84-100; madness, 95-97, 99; dramatic poetry, 100, 104; meditative poetry, 100-103, 134, 155-57; widening vision, 105-108; dance as metaphor, 108-13, 167, 168; idealized woman, 78, 79, 114, 115; love poetry, 117-25; dramatic monologue, 126-40; catalogue device, 131-33; bird imagery, 134, 135, 137, 138; reprise of earlier influences, 141-49; sense of place, 157, 158; metaphysical imagery, 159-63; emblematic imagery, 162, 163; tradition, progressions in development of, 165-68
"Root Cellar," 37, 91
"Rose, The," 157-59

Røstvig, Maren-Sofie, 163
Rothberg, Winterset (Roethke's pseudonym), 53n

"Sale," 7-10
Seager, Allan, 95, 112n, 145
"Sensibility! O La!" 74-80, 83
Sequence, Sometimes Metaphysical, 5, 141, 149, 159-62
Shakespeare, William, 116; *Antony and Cleopatra*, 112, 113; *Richard II*, 29
"Shape of the Fire, The," 47-49, 86n
Shelley, Percy Bysshe, 19, 21, 165, 166; "Adonais," 77n
Sidney, Sir Philip, 109
"Slug," 88
Smart, Christopher, 51-53, 56, 96, 97, 165; "Song to David, A," 51, 52
Snodgrass, W. D., 126
"Some Remarks on Rhythm," 62-64, 86, 131, 133
Spender, Stephen, 3, 4
Spenser, Edmund, 25, 26, 109, 111n
Sterne, Laurence, 76, 77
Stevens, Wallace, 126
Stoner, Winifred Sackville, Jr., 65
Strode, William, 80-82
"Swan, The," 117, 118

Telemachus, 87
"Theodore Roethke Writes . . . ," 108, 126
"This Light," 19, 20
Thomas, Dylan, 52, 53, 149
Thomas, St., 89
Thoreau, Henry, 49
"Tirade Turning, A," 74, 75
"Transplanting," 141n
Truesdale, C. W., 12, 13

"Unfold! Unfold!" 104-106

Vaughan, Henry, 19, 20, 33, 106, 160n; "Retreat, The," 105; "Revival, The," 104, 105; "Vain Wits and Eyes," 160, 161; "Vanity of Spirit," 160n
Verhaeren, Emile, 90
Virgil, 109

Waggoner, Hyatt H., 49n
Wagoner, David, 105n
Wain, John, 24, 126
Waking, The, 106-109, 141n
"Waking, The," 108, 141n
"Weed Puller," 39, 40
"What Can I Tell My Bones?" 132, 135, 139
"Where Knock Is Open Wide," 51-56
Whitman, Walt, 127-41, 144n, 152-54, 165, 167; "After the Supper and Talk," 137; "Noiseless Patient Spider, A," 132, 133; "Out of the Cradle Endlessly Rocking," 128, 135-38; *Sands at Seventy*, 137; "So Long!" 152; "Song of the Broad-Axe," 131, 132; "Song of Myself," 130, 137, 154; "Song of the Open Road," 129, 139; "To Get the Final Lilt of Songs," 129
Williams, William Carlos, 135
Wither, George, 65
Whitney, Geffrey, 162n
Words for the Wind, 117
"Words for the Wind," 117
Wordsworth, William, 24-56, 60, 97, 107, 150, 152, 165, 166; *Borderers The*, 25, 140; *Descriptive Sketches*, 36; "Epistle to Sir George Beaumont," 34; *Excursion, The*, 45, 67-71, 153; "Michael," 30; "Nutting," 25-29; "Old Cumberland Beggar, The," 29, 30; *Prelude, The*, 24, 31-49, 54, 56; "Resolution and Independence," 29, 30; "Return," 41; "Solitary Reaper, The," 12; "Unremitting Voice, The," 37

Wylie, Elinor, 19, 20, 23

Yeats, William Butler, 6, 109-17, 125, 127, 132, 137, 165-68; "Acre of Grass An," 96n; "Among School Children," 109, 113; "Coole Park and Ballylee, 1931," 114, 124; "Lines Written in Dejection," 142 "Magi, The," 143, 144; "Michael Robartes and the Dancer," 124

PRINCETON ESSAYS IN LITERATURE

The Orbit of Thomas Mann. By Erich Kahler

On Four Modern Humanists: Hofmannsthal, Gundolf, Curtius, Kantorowicz. Edited by Arthur R. Evans, Jr.

Flaubert and Joyce: The Rite of Fiction. By Richard Cross

A Stage for Poets: Studies in the Theatre of Hugo and Musset. By Charles Affron

Hofmannsthal's Novel "Andreas." By David H. Miles

Kazantzakis and the Linguistic Revolution in Greek Literature. By Peter Bien

Modern Greek Writers. Edited by Edmund Keeley and Peter Bien

On Gide's *Prométhée*: Private Myth and Public Mystification. By Kurt Weinberg

The Inner Theatre of Recent French Poetry. By Mary Ann Caws

Wallace Stevens and the Symbolist Imagination. By Michel Benamou

Cervantes' Christian Romance: A Study of "Persiles y Sigismunda." By Alban K. Forcione

The Prison-House of Language: a Critical Account of Structuralism and Formalism. By Frederic Jameson

Ezra Pound and the Troubadour Tradition. By Stuart Y. McDougal

Wallace Stevens: Imagination and Faith. By Adalaide K. Morris

On the Art of Medieval Arabic Literature. By Andras Hamori

The Poetic World of Boris Pasternak. By Olga Hughes

The Aesthetics of György Lukács. By Béla Királyfalvi

The Echoing Wood of Theodore Roethke. By Jenijoy La Belle

Library of Congress Cataloging in Publication Data

La Belle, Jenijoy, 1943-
The echoing wood of Theodore Roethke.

(Princeton essays in literature)
Includes index.
1. Roethke, Theodore, 1908-1963—Criticism and interpretation. I. Title.
PS3535.039Z66 811'.5'4 76-3265
ISBN 0-691-06312-5